Facing Death

Worthwhile Reflection on a Necessary Subject

Nelson P. Miller

Facing death: worthwhile reflection on a necessary subject.

Miller, Nelson P.

Published by:

Crown Management LLC – July 2017

1527 Pineridge Drive
Grand Haven, MI 49417
USA

ISBN: 978-0-9980601-6-3

All Rights Reserved
© 2017 Nelson P. Miller
c/o 111 Commerce Avenue S.W.
Grand Rapids, MI 49503
(616) 301-6800 ext. 6963
millern57@gmail.com

For those who expect to die, once.

Table of Contents

Prologue 1
Introduction 6

1   Death and Science 10
2   Death and Medicine 23
3   Death and Consciousness 35
4   Death and Art 50
5   Death and Music 67
6   Death and Culture 78
7   Death and Law 91
8   Death and History 107
9   Death and Philosophy 119
10   Death and Religion 129
11   Death Defeated 143
12   Resurrected Life 154

Conclusion 161
Epilogue 166
Bibliography 169
About the Author 177

Prologue

All share a common destiny—the righteous and the wicked, the good and the bad.... This is the evil in everything that happens under the sun: the same destiny overtakes all. ... For the living know that they will die, but the dead know nothing; they have no further reward, and even their name is forgotten.

Ecclesiastes 9:2-5.

You can't defeat death, we hear. We certainly can't avoid it. In fact, you and I could have died a long time ago. Just think of the highways that you've traveled, motor-vehicle accidents being a leading cause of death. I have been in two major motor-vehicle accidents and drove miraculously right through a third one, stopping to walk back and check on the dead, a young couple. Seeing them crushed side by side into the pancaked little steel-sarcophagus Subaru was incredibly sad, more so because of their youth. The stranger with whom I stood at the driver's side window of the mangled mini-wagon asked me if I thought it was worth checking for a pulse. Regretfully, I shook my head *no*, knowing that the braver thing to do would have been to check myself. He reached in through the shattered window anyway, touching the pale neck of the nearest corpse. Nothing, of course. He didn't bother checking the other one, although also within short reach to both of us. We turned away at once in disgust. About 40,000 people a year were dying on American highways then. The figure dropped for a while but is right back up there, airbags and all.

My father was with me for that drive-through fatal accident. We were following a big Suburban on the freeway when the little mini-wagon came skittering across the median from the other direction. A

Subaru stands no chance in a hundred-mile-an-hour T-bone with a Suburban. Somehow, though, we flew unscathed right through the smoke, vehicles, and debris. Wisely, my father declined to walk back with me to check the dead, although I wish he had. Dads, take every opportunity to punch your man card when you are with your son. Sons always appreciate it, even if doing so may ruin your weekend. We had been going to a jazz festival together, but the accident kind of put a damper on that. Figuring that I was the best eyewitness to the accident, I left my business card with the dad who had been driving the Suburban, as he, his wife, and soon-arriving emergency personnel tended to their scared and injured kids. The wife was hurt badly but ignoring it as she helped her kids. Amazing what moms will do.

You've surely had near misses, too, whether you knew so or not. How many times has the reaper taken a good swing at us but just barely missed, as we moved on blissfully unaware? My two motor-vehicle accidents, ones that I *didn't* somehow escape, were an 18-wheeler to 10-wheeler, a real fandango, and then a 10-wheeler to a 4-wheeler, not quite so big a deal. I was hauling horses in both accidents, and only the horses were hurt, and even somehow not that badly once we got them all untangled. The sleepy trucker who had run over us with his 18-wheeler felt very bad, so bad that he was great help getting the horses lifted off the panels and dividers over which his truck had instantly catapulted them. I felt worse for him, figuring that he was about to lose his job. We all felt worst for the horses because they had nothing to do with it. One second, you're eating hay. The next second, you're hanging over your stall divider. So is life. Yet why, really, must we do life at seventy miles per hour?

If vehicle accidents shouldn't have killed us, then medical conditions should have. After all, how many alarmingly high fevers, severe infections, massive allergic reactions, and other similar medical crises have you had? Way too many, I'm sure. Let's spare one another the old-person drama. Suffice it to say that I have had mostly untreatable, inexplicable reactive blisters over pretty much my entire body, head to toe, *twice.* What's *your* Achilles' heel? The miracle for any of us is that the body works at all, when, oh, once a year or so, it seems to be trying to kill us. Or maybe we're trying to kill *it*, with the stupid habits we demand on pursuing, as if we had the right to kill ourselves and were going to make a very good effort doing so. Sometimes, our bodies seem to be killing us, while other times we seem to be killing our bodies. And not that medicine is the cure-all that we want it to be. Some studies report that tens of thousands die in U.S. hospitals every year *because of* treatment. Doctor, I said the *left* leg, no, no, the *left* leg. I've had a hospital risk manager slap her forehead in disbelief while telling me that they *still* get it wrong even when the patients have written in big marker on the correct limb.

Indeed, other times, others seem to be killing us. Even if we are generally our own worst enemies, we manage to find other enemies, too. I, for instance, really should have died a *very* long time ago. Late in her life, my mother confessed to a reliable relator and friend that she would have aborted me if abortion had then been legal. I was born very shortly after my older brother, while my father was just preparing to enter graduate school and my parents living in married-student housing. Think *two kids in diapers* and *nothing to pay for the diapers*. My artistic mother and ambitious-and-artistic father had great designs on life, as well they should have had, but family must not then have been one of them, as well as they treated me nonetheless. I should have figured that I wasn't the most welcome stranger in the house, but thanks to my parents' generous love, the thought just never occurred to me. I wouldn't be here if I'd been conceived later when abortion was legal and readily available, as my mother later attested. Fifty million-plus American unborn children have since then suffered my near-miss fate.

Many of us, though, probably have the opposite sense, not that we should have died a long time ago but instead that living anything less than a full eighty-year life is to have fate short-change us. Maybe you, like I, just haven't felt so strongly that way and instead have always felt how near death *should* be, even if it necessarily isn't. You've heard of *original sin*, referring to our birth in corruption and corruption throughout body and life? Maybe you are with me in never quite feeling the pride of purity that others seem to feel, unless they're only hiding their realization of the twisted stuff that constitutes them, too. I don't know about you, but my constant decomposition is both physical *and* mental. Our minds are far too often a mess. Oh, we can think clearly of wonderful things, but doing so only reminds us of how *un*wonderful we are. Then there's the body. The darn thing is always a constant challenge, its decomposition for most of us plainly accelerating.

So, my sense is not only that motor-vehicle accidents, medical treatment, family members, or probability should have taken you and me long ago but that *judgment* should have done so, too. As troublesome as we each are, we each seem to be here by the grace of God and overwhelming mercy of many. I don't blame my mother for wanting to have aborted me. She many times later had warrant to take me out back and shoot me, as it is. I can remember her saying so, *I could just shoot you*, sometimes uttering an expletive before or after, not because I was an openly rebellious child, just sullenly so, which of course is the worst type. Don't you feel the same way that to live is mercy and to die would be well-deserved fate? My wife and I have even lived adjacent to a cemetery for about the last thirty years, where the interments have a predictable regularity. Maybe you didn't know that they dig the graves in middle of the night, presumably to respect the sensibilities of the cemetery's daytime visitors. So, death has just always felt familiar to me, even *deserved of* me. That conclusion may sound too morbid for you, which is fine. When death creeps in, with those encounters that we simply cannot avoid, keep looking the other way. You are probably healthier for doing so. Yet familiarity with death, its honest examination, can teach one things. So, thank you for giving me the living chance to share a hopeful reflection on death. You may live better for it.

~

He sat bedside in the nursing home, holding his father's hand as his father lay dying. His father's letter had pretty much put the proverbial nail in his father's literal coffin. He had long prayed that his father would receive the Spirit that would raise his father to eternal glory in Christ. The son had matured in a house that did not know the Spirit, or if it knew, then so firmly rejected Him as to keep anything but the secular forms of Christmas and Easter firmly outside the door. The son, by contrast, had always heard the Spirit's call. Marriage had liberated the son from familial ties enough that he fell into the Lord's sure embrace. The son's life of prayer and petition seemed to do little, though, to free his father for the same glorious end. When father declined sharply toward imminent demise, while manically resisting the son's quiet overtures toward faith, son had finally written father a short letter beseeching a last decision on the fateful question. He left the letter bedside in the nursing home on one of his frequent visits. Father had promptly written back, motioning to son to take the letter from bedside and read it: thanks, but no thanks, not for him, not for his wife, and not for his other son. Within days, his father had fallen into struggling, moaning incomprehension, no longer capable of thought or communication. But then, something had happened, the glorious meaning and incalculable value of which the son instantly knew.

Introduction

Where, O death, is your victory?
Where, O death, is your sting?

1 Corinthians 15:55.

In one word, how do *you* think, or refuse to think, about death? Death *feared* or death *ignored*? Does death *mystify* you, or do you simply *avoid* the thought of death? Maybe, curiously you *countenance* death, bravely you *embrace* death, morbidly you *dwell* on death, or pruriently death *entertains* you. Your approach might be to *outrun* death, which of course you can't, or to *succumb* to death, which of course you can, or to *court* death, which too many of us surely do. If, though, you gave it your best effort, your best thought, your deepest exploration, then how would you, *should* you, come to view death, and on what evidence, to what end, and with what rationale would you so conclude? These are the questions that this book addresses through various perspectives, from science and medicine, through art, music, and culture, to law, history, and philosophy, and finally religion, which more than any form tries to deal most directly with death. You may not have time or inclination to look too closely at death and should certainly not let it lure and entrap you. Yet giving it at least this quick survey glance, and maybe moreover *facing* death even if momentarily, may reveal to you something useful and important that you can still pursue while living. Learn from death how to live.

Funny, but a book on death must be *about the living*. One lives in constant countenance of death, even if we mostly ignore it. Death's frank acknowledgment will always be the most profound aspect of living. I write, in general, only to encourage myself and others. Yet the most encouraging book that one could write would have to be one about death, if to any significant degree such a text answered questions that each of us must hold about death. Indeed, death may be the one subject about which each of us should write. We all have the right, license, and incentive to contemplate death. Death may be the one subject, as Benjamin Franklin observed *along with taxes*, on which we all have equal footing to opine. Somewhere well north of one-hundred billion humans have lived, and all but the current seven-and-a-half billion or so, and maybe a few other ancients depending on your read of history, have died. The odds are not good for avoiding it. I readily admit to having no greater expertise in the subject of death than do you, although I have known and at times retained experts in death, toxicologists, medical examiners, and pediatric oncologists (cancer doctor for kids) among them. The main difference between you and me is likely that I am *recording* the things that you've been thinking or, if not thinking, then wanting or needing to think while instead avoiding them. Let's hope that it helps you that I do so.

Every community has stories of death, although, just as we mostly ignore death, we mostly hide and forget the stories. That's a mistake. The stories tell of the profound. Death *is* profound. We *must* recognize and treat its profundity because we all live, as the Latin proverb goes, with wolves behind and a precipice in front of us. Our stories should include what we have discovered of the profound meaning of death. We see or attempt to see meaning in *everything*, compelled in our best nature to interpret and make sense of the world and our place in it. Or not. Sigmund Freud wrote in *The Letters of Sigmund Freud* that to question the meaning of life is to admit that one is sick. But then, Freud, like other profound thinkers, was wrong about a lot of things. Many others have wrestled deeply with meanings of life and death, and productively so. Cultural anthropologist Ernest Becker, in *The Denial of Death*, maintained that we are unique among animals in wanting to live while knowing of our certain death, producing culture through our manic, anxiety-driven death terror. While Becker's mostly untestable premise may sound overblown, subsequent experiments, recounted in science journalist Dick Teresi's *The Undead*, do suggest that the mere mention of death makes us cling to and defend our affinities and worldviews, no matter what those affinities and worldviews may entail.

In any case, all of us have, at some point, reason to wrestle with death, whether we do so deliberately, reflectively, meditatively, or instead acting out the unanswered question in good or bad habits, mostly the latter. One might think that hospitals, where vast numbers of deaths regularly occur, would be among the institutions most skilled in helping us countenance and deal with death, although that doesn't at all seem so. Instead, we find other institutions, like the local church, that know better how to conceptualize, countenance, and to a degree even accept or embrace death, as regular adherents can attest. In church, under the image of the cross, one has no getting around death, whether Jesus still hangs there in the Catholic tradition or not, in the Protestant. Christ followers embrace death not because of fatalism, guilt, sin, or foolishness, as too many imagine, but instead out of history, hope, and love. We know the God of the living. We know that moralistic therapeutic deism, meaning that *I'm good enough for whatever's out there because I feel good*, is not enough. Such moralism is enough only for as long as one feels good, which is usually not for that long.

Yet even having said so, I don't quite come to you with answers as much as with questions, again questions that you, too, have probably been thinking or perhaps quietly avoiding thinking while knowing that you are doing so. Instead of doctrinal answers, those that may not satisfy your need to explore this one issue that we ultimately must each explore *alone*, this book brings you questions with directions. My research on death and how we think of it reveals that a lot of the things on which we seem popularly to depend, the *I've-got-this-death-thing-figured-out* constructs that many of us regard as solid, reliable, even incontestable by anyone rational and sound, are not there in the form that we think we know them. Life, death, identity, personality, time, passage, purpose—all these things are much more up for grabs than you might have realized. Exploring them anew, even to embrace their unknowable uncertainty long enough to claim a new stance from death, makes for a worthwhile reflection. Join me in that reflection on so necessary of a subject as death.

~

Husband, wife, and young daughter had been attending the African-American, Pentecostal church for a while, where they were the only regular white attendees among the several hundred other members. Then, a beloved elder member who had befriended them, as nearly everyone else in the congregation had made them so dearly welcome, died. They expected a somber or at least sedate memorial service, nothing like the dancing, shouting, running, jumping, and general celebration of the regular evening and Sunday services that they so enjoyed. Their expectations couldn't have been more wrong. If anything, the memorial, billed throughout as a going home celebration, was more joyous than the regular services, itself a feat. The other thing that surprised them, although they should have anticipated it, was the open way in which the pastor exhorted visiting family members, some of whom might not have shared the departed member's faith. Every member trusted where the departed member had gone and knew where those outside the faith would go. The pastor wanted the irregular family members to know that they had the choice, too.

1

Death and Science

> *Who can live and not see death, or who can escape the power of the grave?*
>
> *Psalm 89:48.*

    Surprisingly, theorists reach little consensus on what constitutes either life or death. Life is so varied and subtle that theories of life must focus on properties like the ability to reproduce, adapt to the environment, and self-sustain in metabolic process. Philosophy professor Mark Bedau, co-author of the book *The Nature of Life* and contributor of a chapter by the same name in Steven Luper's *Cambridge Companion to Life and Death*, cites renowned Nobel-winning Austrian physicist Erwin Schrodinger's classic *What Is Life?* for these definitional subtleties. Organisms live when they eat, drink, and breathe, or follow similar metabolic processes to avoid or at least delay decay, while interacting sustainably with their environment. But other factors promptly come into play. Life also implies a single unit of limited duration that can carry information controlling the organism. Growth and stability, in the sense of self-maintaining and self-organizing around relatively constant form, are other critical or typical life attributes. Some theorists define life flexibly by clusters of such attributes, including around a program-metabolism-container model.

    You get the picture: simply defining life is a little more complex than unconsidered thought would have it. The question is important because only the living can die. We do, as philosophy lecturer Christopher Belshaw writes in the book *Annihilation*, use a language of death for the inanimate, speaking of careers, cars, stars, and other lifeless things dying. In Belshaw's loose way of defining it, he, despite his rigorous thought, admitting that we cannot define it strictly, *death* means the irreversible cessation of the living qualities of an organism. And by organism, we tend not to mean an ocean, planet, or ecological system. The reference is instead to an individual, carbon-based, biological entity programmed in some sense by unique DNA-coded genetics connecting the individual entity to other living things. And not just a *part* of an entity, like the living kidney or heart removed from a dead donor for prompt transplant into a living recipient, but instead a whole organism capable of continued life.

Recognizing who is a person, *human* life, introduces other complexities. Philosophy professor Eric Olson, author of the chapter *What Are We?* in the same *Cambridge Companion* compendium, begins with human life implicating a member of the homo-sapiens primate species, having the potential for intelligent self-reflection, as key attributes. Yet he usefully discerns that this animalism/species definition misses an important personal-identity point. We would not be who we are if, for instance, we had a brain transplant. Isn't who any individual is bound up in the unique collection of memories, thoughts, character, and disposition, locally in the brain, more so than in the whole organism? And yet not even in the brain because if we could engineer transferring one's conscious sense of self and will from the brain, letting brain die, into another brain or even an artificial brain, wouldn't *that* conscious will in some sense be *us*?

While the answers to these critical questions are not crystal clear, they do suggest that *humanness* has something uniquely to do with experience and identity quite apart from the organism. Human life has more to do with individual, continuous consciousness, unique personal sentience, than it does with animal-bound organic life. Hoping to minimize metaphysics and eschew spirituality, theoreticians like Olson wish to avoid the mind-body dualism that these thought experiments entail. They would, their writings and secular stances suggest, prefer to treat human life as animal life, solely material rather than distinctly personal and conscious, and thus in some sense necessarily metaphysical. Yet they are largely unable to fold human life into conventional theories of life in general. Thinking, Olson concludes, is logically either incompatible with the material or incompatible with being biologically alive.

Scientific conceptions of time do not necessarily help how we should understand living and dying. Time binds the concepts of life and death. To live is to persist over time, while to die is for that time of living to reach its end in time. Yet persistence is itself a difficult logical puzzle about which theoreticians disagree, as professor of philosophy Katherine Hawley, author of the book *How Things Persist*, writes in the chapter *Persistence and Time* in the above *Cambridge Companion*. Things in space can certainly exist while quite apart. You, the reader, exist some distance from me, the writer, each real but distant in space. In time, though, as events occur in the present and pass into the past, do they continue to exist, or are they gone? They happened once, but after happening, do they remain real? The future raises similar questions. Things that haven't happened yet don't exist, or do they? Once they happen, they are certain to have come to pass because they *did* happen. Does that mean that they existed in the future? You may think that I am playing tricks on you, but theories of time wrestle so deeply with these questions as to divide into not just two but three different camps, some saying that things only exist in the present, others saying that things exist in the future, present, and past, and still others holding that nothing exists in the future but only in the present and past. Notice that two of these three theories have a sort of *eternalism* to them, using time-theoretician Hawley's term, things existing either before they occur or after they have passed, or both.

Defining death relative to time gets harder, not easier, when we inject a single persistent person into the time equation. Are you who you were yesterday and will be tomorrow? In other words, do you endure as a physical, conscious, and spiritual being through time? The material constituting your body changes over time. You are not the blood, water, and tissue that you were once were, a difference that doesn't seem to matter because you still think as the same person who you were. Or do you? You probably don't think, act, react, experience, will, and emote as you once did, even if memories and mannerisms persist. Ask your friends, and you won't even get the same answer whether they think that you or they are the same persons whom you once were. Recall, too, that because of disease or injury some persons lose all sense of prior self, becoming in character, skill, experience, and memory, if not bodily, a new person. In each case, the former and present person both certainly existed. Whether they both still exist depends on your view of time, whether the problematic *presentism* or alternative *eternalism*.

These explorations raise the question of the *malleability of identity*, treated in a *Cambridge Companion* chapter of that name by the philosophy professor Marya Schechtman. You can see how the question of personal identity, like the question of persistence through time, informs the question of life and death. Has the former person whose disease or injury eliminated all memory and character in some sense died, reborn in the developing new self? Indeed, can individuals without disease or injury experience such extensive transformation of identity and character as to be new persons? Schechtman concludes that personal identity, both literal and figurative, is more malleable than we think. The question of personal persistence through time up to death, and what to make of personal identity after death, isn't quite so simple even, or especially, from a strictly theoretical point of view.

The question of the event or moment of death may also be less clear and more complex than we commonly think, as the following paragraphs show, because of the difficulty we face in defining just what constitutes *death*. As Edgar Allan Poe wrote in 1884's *The Premature Burial*, the "boundaries which divide Life from Death are at best shadowy and vague. Who shall say where one ends, and where the other begins?" Because of those definitional problems, research scientist P-L Chau and law fellow Jonathan Herring, in the chapter *The Meaning of Death* in the book *Death Rites and Rights*, see death as more of a process than event. A person may die socially or emotionally at one moment, mentally or cognitively at another, physiologically or biologically at another, and legally, theologically, or spiritually at other moments. If so, then a person may at times be alive for one purpose, say, anatomically for transplant, when dead for another purpose, say, legally for authorization of the same, as legal theorist Elizabeth Price Foley points out in her book *The Law of Life and Death*. Indeed, scientists also perceive developmental continuity at life's beginning, rather than one clear starting point for life, Chau and Herring note, and biological continuity across generations after an individual's death. They add that a dead person's body parts may persist biologically in transplant and even a dead person's identity in the case of face transplants. So, they ask, why should scientists not also treat biological death as an ambiguous process rather than an event?

The nature of death may also be more complex than we think. Science leads us not to a single definition of death but to several definitions, each presenting theoretical, practical, social, legal, and moral problems. Bioethics researcher David DeGrazia, in the chapter *The Nature of Human Death* in the *Cambridge Companion*, reminds us of the mainstream whole-brain standard for death. Death occurs, the mainstream of medicine accepts, when the whole brain including brain stem suffers irreversible cessation of function. Widespread belief is that this whole-brain standard took the place of an earlier cardiopulmonary standard under which life ended and death occurred with irreversible cessation of heart and lung function. Medical advances like artificial respiration made the old heart-lung standard obsolete. Technology could keep a person alive, thinking, conscious, and willing, with artificial heart and lung support. With technological life support available, natural cardiopulmonary cessation was not sufficient to call one dead, when the brain and stem were still functioning well enough not just to direct other systems but even for consciousness. A person could live with machines providing heart and lung function. Brain death seemed to make more sense.

A chapter below on the history of death, though, shows that since the ancients, examiners have been wary of relying on the appearance that breathing and heartbeat have stopped, as reliable indicators of death. A strict cardiopulmonary standard, societies have long known, leads to way too many mistakes in declaring death, when even one or two mistakes is too many. Remember, too, that the traditional standard involved *irreversible* cardiopulmonary loss. If resuscitation efforts could restore heart and lung function that had already stopped, then the patient would not have been dead. Rigor mortis, meaning a stiffening of the muscles, algor mortis, meaning a temperature fall until it reaches ambience, liver mortis, meaning skin discoloration from uncirculated blood, and decomposition were the more-reliable signs that examiners used right into the twentieth century. Heart and lung function has certainly stopped irreversibly when those conditions are clear.

The clear modern trend, though, is exactly the opposite, not to wait for rigor mortis to set in to confirm that a person has died but instead to declare a person dead not only when their body is alive but also when their brain is active. The mainstream whole-brain standard is under sharp attack from higher-brain advocates who would call death the irreversible loss of capacity for consciousness. To these advocates, *some* brain activity is not enough to claim a person as alive. Instead, *higher* brain activity must be the minimum. Chau and Herring in their chapter *The Meaning of Death* note those who advocate for two death standards, one like the rigor-mortis standard for death of the human organism and the other like the irreversible-loss-of-consciousness standard for death of the person. Those who advocate for multiple standards also advocate that only the latter standard, the personhood standard dependent on consciousness, implicates moral and ethical concerns.

For his part, bioethics researcher DeGrazia argues weakly for a fourth circulatory-respiratory standard, not that one lives or dies based on brain function or even heart or lung function but on the capacity for circulatory and respiratory function. In doing so, he concludes that differences among the three more-modern standards defining death may only be quibbles, advocating instead that physicians should get to terminate care for any irreversibly unconscious patient who had failed to demand continued care and accumulated the funds to pay for it. Should we ask here why ethicists, of all professionals, should be the ones who so often seem so willing to cross traditional ethical lines, giving power to presumed experts over the lives of others? A pattern one also sees is that to do so, ethicists first reject anything transcendent in human existence and thus any sanctity or inherent worth in the individual. Every material rationalization, such as that persons have protectible value only when conscious or financially able, readily follows. Ethicists are no more ethical than anyone else once they reject the only foundation for ethics, which necessarily lies in the transcendent and intrinsic.

Cultural anthropologist Donald Joralemon reports in *Moral Dilemmas*, though, some interesting history in American medicine's move from cardiopulmonary to brain-death standards. Yes, heart-lung machines were newly keeping patients alive, but some of those patients had no brain function, which hardly seemed like living. Then, South African surgeon Christian Barnard famously performed the first heart transplant in the late 1960s, when cardiopulmonary function still defined death. Dr. Barnard had taken a beating heart out of the donor, a young woman severely brain-injured in a motor-vehicle accident, as would be necessary for heart transplants. Medicine needed a new definition of death if it was going to perform heart transplants taking a living heart out of a brain-dead patient. With the advance of mechanical ventilators keeping alive patients without the brain function to sustain their own breathing, Harvard Medical School had already planned a committee to address the issue of whether the medical community could define and treat these patients as dead.

Perhaps unfortunately, or if not that, then too frankly and transparently, in its report the committee stated that its purpose in adopting a new definition of death was not merely to guide physicians, lawyers, and courts in how medical-care providers treated the breathing-alive but brain-dead patient. Rather, or in addition, the committee stated that its purpose was to facilitate organ transplants, not so much that physicians needed a safe harbor for patient care but that someone needed organs. In any case, the committee's report substituted a brain-death standard for the former cardiopulmonary standard. The American public accepted the brain-death standard with little resistance, although recent cases have brought the standard into public view once again, this time with greater controversy than the standard's initial adoption produced.

A problem with the brain-death standard is that brain death is not readily observable. Oh, sure, electroencephalographs (EEGs) and other tests can measure brain waves. And the initial Harvard-committee proposal included among its four criteria for determining death under the new definition that physicians perform two EEGs twenty-four hours apart, finding no brain waves, before a declaration of brain death. Everyone, including otherwise credible experts in related fields, assumes that hospitals are performing these EEGs on patients who may or may not be dead. Trouble is, few are. Organ harvesting routinely goes on from the purportedly brain dead without any EEG or similar test for brain waves. Instead, the current brain-death standard widely in use permits a single examiner to make reflex tests of eyes, ears, and throat to call it brain death, when highly credible studies show that it often isn't. Hospitals routinely use the modified-Harvard standard that if the body doesn't blink, gag, cough, or shiver, and the eyes roll when tipped, then the person is *brain dead*, without any check at all for brain waves, even though the public believes that hospitals are checking for brain waves. For confirmation, read cardiologist/medical professor Haider Warraich's account, in his book *Modern Death*, of how brief and simple a procedure it was, the first time that he ever declared a patient dead, following the hospital's short checklist. Feel for a pulse, listen for a heartbeat, poke the eye (that's the brain-death part of confirming no reflex), and he was done. Long gone, in the interest of organ harvesting, is any sort of putrefaction standard, as used throughout the ages, no less an EEG testing for brain waves.

Read science journalist Dick Teresi's research, in his book *The Undead*, on the organ-harvesting industry, to see how medicine can, even with skilled professionals possessed of the best of intentions, blur the line between life and death. Teresi, former editor of Science Digest and Omni magazines, reports that individuals declared brain dead and ready for organ transplant have revived, even with minimal effects. Or consider legal theorist Elizabeth Price Foley's description, in her book *The Law of Life and Death*, of how, to harvest healthy organs, physicians carefully orchestrate a controlled cardiopulmonary death of brain-*living* patients whose advance medical directives refuse unwanted treatment. Foley highlights the ethical concerns of this practice of hastening the death of a living patient to harvest organs, citing ethicist Arthur Caplan who calls the controversial procedure *snatch and grab*. After all, how can physicians declare dead the brain-living patient whose cardiopulmonary death they have just brought about with cessation of treatment, when they then promptly *restart* the heart and lung function after controlled cessation? Death is supposed to be irreversible. Isn't the patient once again, or still, *living* as soon as the heart and lungs restart, meaning that the harvesting is arguably from a *living* rather than dead person?

Foley also examines how physicians may be *inducing* controlled death, rather than simply withdrawing treatment to orchestrate controlled death, to prepare for organ harvest, using a mix of painkiller, muscle relaxer, blood thinner, and anti-anxiety medicines, each of which physicians regularly use for therapeutic treatment of living patients under similar treatment circumstances. In other words, drugs used to save can have the double effect of drugs used to kill. Foley recounts the criminal trial of a transplant surgeon who had administered large doses of those drugs to a patient whose family had consented to controlled death and organ harvest. The patient somehow fought off the effect of the large doses, surviving too long for organ harvest but then dying shortly later, allegedly due to the drug overdoses. The state charged the surgeon with hastening the death, but the jury acquitted. The use of therapeutic drugs in this setting blurs the line between inducing death, still prohibited in theory, and orchestrating death under control, as widely permitted. While some would say that we are going too far, others would say that we have not gone far enough. Foley reports advocacy to abandon the dead-donor rule. Foley further reports that one state is planning to extend to settings outside of the hospital, the practice of declaring cardiopulmonary death and then quickly starting organ-preservation procedures so that attendants can get the healthy organs, and ostensibly dead person, back to the hospital for harvesting.

These concerns show that when considering what death is from a scientific and material perspective alone, we must distinguish between definitions, like Belshaw's irreversible cessation of the living qualities of an organism, from criteria and tests for death, like the cardiopulmonary or brain-death standards. We must also be aware of the incentives that the standards create and who, or what, are the winners and losers. Moreover, the thing about which to be cautious in scientific interpretations of death is not to take the science farther than science goes. Science is a method devoted to material questions and, yes, an extraordinarily *powerful* and even *beautiful* method. Science is not, on the other hand, a transcendent explanation, philosophy, or end. The questions of life and death are both physical and *meta*physical, both biological *and* ethical, with science addressing only the former in each case, not the latter.

One begets scien*tism* when making of science a metaphysical philosophy or transcendent end. Science tests theories, accepting the theory as empirically verified when it is consistent with test results and more reasonably explanatory and predictive than any other known theory. Science, both logic and history have proven, is always a matter of being the best that we can do until inquiry and verification produce a stronger theory. Science thus does not *prove incontestable truths* but instead *verifies premises* that scientists continue to constantly and properly contest, even while accepting those premises as currently reliable. Science represents a kind of thoughtful rationalism. Yet as a closed system, examining only material things from within a materialist perspective, science cannot address nonmaterial things from which the material first arose and that continue to influence it. Science can project only a material future governed from within its material bounds.

To illustrate science's bounds and rescue us from a blinding scient*ism*, Oxford philosopher Richard Swinburne in his book *Is There a God?* extends science's thoughtful rationalism to testing the proposition for a benevolent, all-powerful creator. The God premise might have us find a universe created out of the nothingness of the cosmologist's singularity, with the physicist's perfectly orderly and exquisitely tuned natural laws arising instantly after the big-bang creation, just as we find. We might also find creatures capable of reflecting with scientific accuracy and moral wonder on God's perfect designs, while possessed of hearts hungry for his love and minds desperate to make meaning of their own ends and his ends. Swinburne concludes that the God premise explains these conditions more rationally than any competing premise such as a materialist's probabilistic randomness. We find no proof of God only in the sense that we find no proof of scientific premises. Yet, as we properly sort the contradictory and competing claims of existentialism, philosophical naturalism, materialism, spirituality, and specific faiths, using our powerful but still-limited rationality, one may rationally find plenty of evidence for God, more so than for God's absence.

Scientism, purporting to extend the methods of science beyond their material bounds to the immaterial and spiritual, nevertheless captures the imagination of many. For example, philosophy professor John Messerly in his book *The Meaning of Life* suggests a scientism view when writing that we *were forged* through mutations and natural selection, making evolution-as-the-forger the *indispensable consideration* for the meaning of life. Messerly's allusion to forging, a human design process, highlights a curious aspect of evolutionary theory when applied popularly beyond its scientific bounds. The popularized theory denies a designer but promptly injects design, here, a *forger*. Scientism implies that organisms, even utterly unthinking single-cell organisms, no less *inanimate* systems in some instances, deliberately, wisely, and effectively pursue ends, even if those ends are only their own increasing complexity in design. That odd supposition of mindless purpose, initiative, and ends is so fantastic as to be farcical. At least the religious ascribe design to a designer. Evolution is a beautiful and powerful theory but then a powerful delusion when scientism ascribes design to it that, as a theory alone, it cannot have, theories having no sentience. Scientism plays god.

Yet even though playing god, scientism admits that without the possibility of escaping death, life and death remain largely or entirely meaningless. How, then, does scientism respond to the fact of death? For some, the technological advances that science promotes supply the answer. Humans will some day live forever, scientism asserts, whether through solving the biological riddle of aging or, if not, then by facilitating uploading of identity and memory from mind to microchip, creating for one's self a sort of virtual eternity. Scientism invites the adherent to anticipate the possibility of material solutions to death, within what scientism holds is a solely material universe. If within a solely material world defeating death metaphysically is impossible, then scientism must defeat death physically, within the bounds of the material universe.

And so, while most scientists tend to hold that science has nothing to say about the metaphysics of life after death, that limitation does not hold true for all of them. In *Physics of the Soul*, quantum physicist Amit Goswami purports to deploy quantum physics in support of theories of immortality and transcendence, arguing that quantum physics supports traditional spiritual and religious beliefs. Debate over the putative connection first arose a hundred years ago, if you can believe it, between the curious Erwin Schrodinger and entirely skeptical Albert Einstein and Max Planck. Today, consensus treats the idea as only quantum *mysticism*, a sort of new-age coloring of religion with the language, if not the rigor and methods, of science. Quantum physics does recognize nonlocal action, meaning that reactions between particles can occur across unfathomably vast distance without sensible material connection. Yet scientific consensus holds that extending quantum concepts into immaterial being takes a leap more like faith than science. Science has its place, as reason both supports and limits it, just as metaphysics, or faith in higher order, supports reason. Science informs us about material and testable aspects of death, not all that we need to learn of it.

~

Although she knew that she was dying, she seemed to her visitors to welcome death. Indeed, she *did* welcome death because she knew that dying meant joining her glorious Savior. Visiting her daily in the hospital, her devoted sister witnessed her growing excitement, even as her sister witnessed her physical decline. Yet even as her physical struggles grew, her anticipation of leaving those struggles for the embrace of her Lord grew so strong and evident that her excitement was contagious. The few intimates who visited left in tears of joy. Word spread quickly of her infectious faith. Then, the most remarkable event happened not just once but on her sister's last three visits. Angels hovered in the room, not caricature cherubic baby angels or spectral visions but instead glorified beings, ignoring the sister and other intimate visitors while rejoicing to take their charge.

2

Death and Medicine

I am overwhelmed with troubles and my life draws near to death.

Psalm 88:3.

Medical school doesn't generally prepare physicians to deal with patient mortality, writes surgeon and medical-school professor Atul Gawande in *Being Mortal*. On dealing with patient death, Gawande recalls only a brief, one-hour study of Tolstoy's *The Death of Ivan Ilych*, in a medical-school seminar on how to relate to a patient. Gawande feels that physicians today, outside of geriatric specialties, may do worse in helping patients countenance their death than did their medical forebears. Medical advances have greatly extended life but simultaneously shifted management of aging and dying from the patient to the professional. Up until the second half of the last century, most Americans died at home. Nearer the end of the last century, fewer than one out of five were doing so. Between fifty and sixty percent of Americans die in hospitals, and many more in nursing homes or other transitional facilities. Americans' fierce and usually healthy commitment to individualism and independence hits a medical brick wall as decline leads to dependence approaching death in the professional's hands.

Gawande helpfully charts this new medical course of decline. Before the advent of modern medicine, personal health would simply fall off the proverbial cliff. One day, you were fine. The next day, you were dead. Life lengthened as medical care improved, but the pattern of life also changed. Diagnoses that would once have been terminal instead became smaller cliffs, enough to catch one's self and return to reasonable health until another small cliff came along, each drop bringing one closer to final demise. Modern medicine comes closer to eliminating all cliffs so that more persons die simply of old age rather than sudden illness and precipitous decline. The new pattern, while a great boon in general, affects the way in which many of us must countenance death, not as an enemy whose sudden attack lays one low but instead as a subtle creeper, stealing little bits of life until the end. Death becomes, as Gawande puts it, the story of our parts wearing out bit by bit until their cumulative decline fells the whole. We wear out rather than disease killing us or even genetics term-limiting us out.

Death seems a very different enemy in this new medical context, indeed less like an enemy and more often like a long-time companion if never quite a friend. Gawande notes in *Being Mortal* that in these long, slow declines, we pursue achievement less, focus on the present over the future, and accept being rather than doing. Our worlds narrow to family and long-time friends. Yet Gawande reports study showing that the elderly experience greater happiness, with less anxiety and depression. Living becomes more emotionally satisfying and less stressful, with calm and wisdom accumulating with age. Yet other than prolonging life and improving its quality, medicine's prowess doesn't particularly help the elderly with the question of mortality. The prowess becomes medicine's point when prowess can only delay, not eliminate, death. Medicine's prowess simultaneously deprives the patient of the autonomy, will, and control that are so important to meaningful life. Medicine even deprives us of our last words and embraces, making death not a noticeable event but a judgment of what medical services to offer and withdraw long past the opportunity for last words and embraces. I held my father's hand the moment that he died, but within the medical context, my doing so seemed pure happenstance.

Hospice, Gawande notes, has recovered from medical science some of dying's humanity. Medicine, using major surgeries, sustaining medical equipment, and arduous drug courses, tends to sacrifice ability now for extended health later. Hospice focuses instead on pain control and family or community environment through dying's process, leaving to medicine concern for the patient's prospects for recovery. Hospice's third commitment after pain relief and social context is to engage the person's spirituality, discussed in a later chapter. Interestingly, hospice's effort to reduce pain and increase autonomy can have beneficial effects on medical health, too. Some see hospice as a death sentence, and indeed, hospice care has in many cases depended on withdrawal of medical care. Not surprisingly, Gawande cites studies indicating that patients are far more willing to accept hospice when assured that they will lose no medical care. The surprising outcomes of concurrent medical-and-hospice care, though, have been substantial reductions in cost and usage of intensive therapies, even as patients lived longer and died more peacefully. Researchers connect at least some of those improved outcomes with the open discussions of dying and death that palliative care encourages or requires.

Medical advance directives encourage those helpful discussions about the process of dying, before its terminal events intercede. Studies of correlations between death rates and holidays or other special events suggest that individuals may to some degree influence physiologically the timing of their death. Advance directives are clearer and more-direct ways of doing so, by directing medical decisions. Simply asking hospital patients at admittance if they want antibiotics, heart resuscitation, intubation for ventilation, and intravenous or tube feeding is enough to stimulate important family conversations. The directives help the medical-care providers, surely, but the conversations also help the patients and their family members and confidantes. One offshoot of these conversations is that the percentage of persons dying at home has reversed its long decline and is instead increasing. We do not institutionalize the dying as much as we once did, instead preserving more autonomy, familiarity, and social support. This recovery of our end, the re-context of our dying, may be especially important in that we tend to judge the quality of anything, whether of a life or meal or cinema experience, by how it ends. The course of an experience is important, but its end takes on outsize significance. To die well is to have lived well, more than we might suspect. Indeed, as Gawande puts it, recognizing and embracing one's finitude can be a final gift. The physician's duty is not, he writes, to ensure survival but instead to enable well-being, including supporting the reasons why one should live.

The advance directives that patients dictate for their doctors and other medical-care providers to follow often provide for do-not-resuscitate orders, as a defense to the overwhelming and invasive technology available to extend less-than-meaningful life. To some degree, we should get to influence the conditions of our imminent demise, whether on a ventilator with intubation or free of those and other invasive encumbrances. Do-not-resuscitate orders place the dignitary control and autonomy rights back in the hands of the individual patient. Or do they? Legal theorist Elizabeth Price Foley in her book *The Law of Life and Death* notes a contrary trend, passing under the rubric of the *futility* doctrine, that is placing greater control in the hands of physicians. If, the trend asks, patients can issue do-not-resuscitate commands, taking into their own hands the question of life and death, then why, under appropriate conditions, shouldn't physicians likewise be able to do so?

Those who value personal autonomy would answer that the person dying should get to decide, but proponents of the contrary trend note the burden on the community of caring for the dying. They advocate a *communitarian* view that the community, typically represented by the physician and an ethics committee, should have a say in the decision whether to resuscitate, no matter what the patient directs. A uniform act adopted or mimicked in several states thus grants physicians the right to refuse care when providing it would be futile, leaving to the physicians defining *futile*. The laws offer some safeguards including giving the family of the patient whose care the physicians plan to terminate a few days to obtain a transfer at the family's expense to a facility willing to provide care, if one exists. Under the laws, physicians and ethics committees are denying care to patients, and hastening the death of patients, whose advance directives request all available care and whose families likewise request it. If do-not-resuscitate is good for the patient, then policy has judged it good, too, for the physician. The power of life and death lies in a balance somewhere between the patient and the community.

Legal theorist Foley also reminds us that many approach death without having thought about end-of-life care and so without a medical advance directive in place. In those cases, medical-care providers turn to family members or other guardians to guide the course of end-of-life care consistent with what those guardians discern that the incompetent patient would have wished. Law supports that process. In doubtful or disputed cases, medical-care providers may turn to hospital legal counsel who may swiftly take the question of care to the local court for hearing. Guardian, family members, friends, and medical-care providers may all testify, ensuring due process over the life-and-death question of care. State law may require a heightened clear-and-convincing evidence standard for removing life support, giving greater assurance of integrity to the process, even if still a daunting degree of state control over the most important of all decisions. The public scrutinizes closely periodic difficult, even notorious disputed cases, sometimes affecting law and policy, although many other questionable cases pass without such scrutiny or reform.

When we think of death, we often think of its causes, which are many, some of them traumatic and sudden, and others chronic, creeping, and subtle. Yet the biggest killer may be life itself, or the limits to life that the human organism naturally faces, what we call *growing old*, or the *process of aging*. Surgeon and medical professor Sherwin Nuland made concerted effort to demystify death in his book *How We Die: Reflections on Life's Final Chapter*. One of his central efforts was to show, by study and personal experience, that although medical examiners must list a specific cause on the certifying record of death, the causes often listed are only the immediate, nearly incidental triggers to a death that was imminent and inevitable. With the accumulating defects and deficits of the naturally aging body, the last-straw trigger could have been anything, but the examiner dutifully lists the one tumor, aneurysm, or infection that they find most obvious out of the several or dozens that they could have chosen. Diseases don't exactly kill us. We might have overcome every single one, except that our increasingly decrepit bodies gradually lose the capacity to overcome any of them, even the least of them. That increasing defenselessness is why the old should get flu shots.

Why, though, do we age to the point of death? Why must we eventually submit to rather than escape death? A current answer, better than any that preceded it, is that our chromosomes permit cell replication only about fifty times before the replication process, after which the chromosome's ends (*telomeres*, if you want to know the term) have worn away, leaving the hazard of incomplete copying. Cells, not in all organisms but in the vast classification of organisms to which we and nearly all other things that we recognize as living beings belong, lose their ability to reproduce. We end up stuck with too many of our body's trillions of cells unable to replicate. We accumulate more and more of the old, worn out cells, until we lose the capacity for continued life, finally felled by something as innocuous as the common cold or even a sneeze that goes along with it. Cardiologist/medical professor Haider Warraich further details in his book *Modern Death* how cells trigger their own deaths when detecting cell damage, a process certain defects in which contributes to half of all cancers. Our cells sometimes kill us.

Environment, diet, exercise, lifestyle, stress, disease, violence, and other factors all may affect life expectancy, but the human population still faces an upper limit to aging. We believe today that the limit is around one-hundred-fifteen to one-hundred-twenty years and that the limit has remained relatively stable over the long term. Yes, life expectancy has improved, especially in developed societies, but longevity has not. Global average life expectancy at birth is now sixty-six years. More of us live longer than most of us used to live, but none of us live longer than anyone once lived, if that makes sense. Warraich reports that the main reason that life expectancies have improved, especially in developed countries, is that child mortality has fallen dramatically. Thankfully, we are saving the children, although not as much our aged selves. Even if no one at all died under age fifty in the United States, when under-fifty deaths currently account for about twelve percent of deaths, life expectancy would only increase another 3.5 years.

In many nations, medical and epidemiological advances have saved most of those whom we can save, although variations continue to exist. For example, Sierra Leone has an average life expectancy of just thirty-four years, contrasted with Japan's life expectancy of eighty-two years. The World Health Organization predicts that local improvements will gradually increase the global average to seventy-three years. Yet other than for local conditions, don't expect life expectancy to continue to improve dramatically in coming years. The trend may already be modestly in the opposite direction for at least some groups. And no matter how much or little are the improvements in life expectancy, longevity limits will likely always remain. Even Methuselah, the oldest Bible figure, living to 969 years, eventually aged out.

As recently as the beginning of the last century, infections killed more than anything else. Antibiotics, vaccinations, and improved hygiene, sanitation, and food distribution, along with other medical and epidemiological advances, have helped to move infectious disease down the cause-of-death list. Warraich reports that in the United States, pneumonia, ranked as only the eleventh-deadliest killer, is the highest infectious disease on the list. Non-infectious processes, most associated with aging, like heart disease, stroke, lung and colon cancer, chronic obstructive lung disease, and diabetes, now lead the list. While worsening lifestyles have contributed to increases in some of these diseases, their increases are also attributable in part to the *reduction* in infectious and other non-aging-related causes. Warraich reports, for instance, that cancer in 1812 in Boston, where records of death were good for the time, may have caused just one half of one percent of deaths, while cancer now causes about 22.5% of U.S. deaths, as the second-leading cause of death. In short, more of us are dying of conditions associated with old age. Death is a condition to which we must prepare to submit, or we will die unprepared.

While death entails a profound submission, some nonetheless try to cheat death. I have already mentioned the cryogenics example, freezing one's self in the hope of revivification ages later when technology might somehow make it possible. Biomedical gerontologist Aubrey de Grey asserts, as reported in the introduction to *Biopolitics and the Philosophy of Death*, that with recent and anticipated advances in the study of aging, the first person to live to a thousand is a surely already alive today and may even already be age sixty. Companies promote to consumers purported ways to save your telomeres, as if we might slow or defeat death, cell by cell at the chromosome level. Philosophy lecturer Belshaw and others discuss other cheating-death approaches, for now more like thought experiments than realistic possibilities, like head swaps, brain transplants, brain downloads for programming of cyborgs and androids, or even disembodied mind or virtual consciousness held in field or other animation. Some think that these surviving entities would have so little of their former person's identity that they would be new rather than old lives. Others are less concerned with continuous identity. Don't we, after all, wake up each morning a little different than who or what we were when we fell asleep? One hears others speak of being a different person, for better or worse, after a certain traumatic, transformative, educational, or inspirational encounter or experience. Those claims are, though, solely or primarily figures of speech because life does seem essentially identified with the single body, the biological organism that sustains consciousness, soul, or spirit.

Death today tries to demand a different kind of submission that it hadn't previously demanded. Everyone recognizes that medical advances tend strongly to shift control over the process of dying from patient to physician. Medicine prolongs life but only or primarily when the medical providers are in control of the sophisticated medical regimens necessary to do so. Dying patients live on at the mercy of invasive devices and debilitating drugs, and those who administer and control them. Dying today demands submission to expertise. Doctors write the death script, when one used to play a primary or significant role in scripting one's own death. Thus, a different way in which those who are dying try not so much to cheat but at least to control death, wiser than decapitation for cryogenic preservation or suspended animation of the head, is to take back the death script. More of the elderly find more support from care providers, both medical and family, for choosing what treatments to forgo and where to end life. With increasing acceptance of patient-approved do-not-resuscitate and do-not-intubate orders, some even manage meaningful last words and last scenes, as they much more often once did.

The medical questions that death raises certainly include the quality of one's life and degree of one's health, as medicine promotes and supports it nearing death. The thought of death makes us measure our lives, and part of that measuring involves our medical health and welfare. How am I today, and how will I be tomorrow, if tomorrow comes for me? Illness brings death to mind, helping us to count and measure our days, especially when the illness is serious or terminal. The measuring involves more, though, than the prospect for continued, reasonably healthy life. Poor health and impending death help us evaluate what we *made* of life and what life made of us, no matter the course of our demise. Ethicist Noah Lemos, in the chapter *Assessing Lives* out of Steven Luper's *Cambridge Companion of Life and Death*, suggests that the joyful and gentle St. Francis might, as he realized that he was dying, have looked back with greater confidence on his life than, say, Hitler or Stalin would look back on the devastation that their lives wrought. A life's quality has more to do with virtuous choices over life's course than the good health in which we live life or the medical course of our demise. Living a *good* life must mean more than living a *healthy* life up to its end. A good life has a necessarily virtuous quality to it.

Pain and illness as one approaches death, though, can surely affect the quality of living and experience of dying, giving end-of-life medical care a peculiarly significant role. Philosophy professor John Martin Fischer, who is editor of the book *The Metaphysics of Death*, points out in his chapter *Mortal Harm* in the *Cambridge Companion* that when we refer to *death,* we may mean any one of three things starting with the process of dying, or the event of death itself, or instead the fact of being dead. The process of dying can be painful or pain free. It can also be swift and unexpected, even not experienced at all as one dies while asleep, or slow and fully anticipated. Listen to people speak about death, and you can see that these variables in the countenance of death affect how we think about the subject. Yet no matter swift or slow, expected or unexpected, the event and manner of death also influence our view of the subject. To die of natural causes seems quite different than to die at the hand of another or at one's own hand. And we even distinguish rather sharply among natural causes when thinking about death, pneumonia being different somehow than cancer or a brain bleed following a fall down stairs.

While these questions of the process of dying and manner of death are important, in the bigger picture, the third meaning of death, of no longer being alive, is the subject that all thinking persons must somehow parse. The process of dying can affect one's life, as can the manner and event of death itself, but being gone from the body is the subject's more-significant part. Here, on the question of no longer being alive in the natural body, the first thought seems to be that death is ordinarily a bad thing, indeed the ultimate loss to life and health. But questions promptly arise that death in at least some cases and perhaps many cases may be a good rather than bad thing, a relieving or otherwise welcome event. You pick the circumstances: relentless untreatable pain; terminal illness with invasive medical care; severe disability; harsh inescapable deprivation; loss of independence or even of sentience; or simply a full life, well lived, with a sense that the time has arrived to go. These or other circumstances may properly affect decisions about end-of-life medical care. Life-extending but painfully invasive care, the classic instance being cardiopulmonary resuscitation, that is fully appropriate in one circumstance may be inappropriate in another circumstance, depending on the trajectory of the patient's life.

We thus appropriately give due thought to medical care approaching death, in the context of the life that we have lived. Indeed, decisions about medical care approaching death demand that we lay a solid foundation for facing death in reckoning of a life. A day long ago might have been when one could just die without deciding on medical care approaching death. That day is long past. Because medical care to extend life is available, medical technology forces on us decisions that we long ago need not have made. A consequence of medical improvements is the need to decide whether to accept them and on what terms. Decisions demand rationales, and rationales demand foundations. As medicine forces us to decide, we must to some degree think about and express our justifications for deciding. You don't see patients and their families flipping coins to decide whether to resuscitate. And as we express our justifications, what we think of who we are becomes clearer and clearer. Our medical decisions nearing death inevitably reveal what we think about living and dying. One who has given no thought to the meaning of living, dying, and death may find harrowing, trying to make those decisions. If we are to die with any grace, if we are to ease the passage not only for ourselves but for those who care for us, then we should develop that foundation well before we enter the medical phase of dying.

Thus, what the above survey of medical and health issues affecting dying may show more than anything is that the primary rationales for medical decision making approaching death lie *outside of medicine*. Yes, what medicine makes possible is important. The course of medical care, including how it affects both the health in which we live and the delay and conditions of our death, is important. We should listen carefully to our doctors and to the medical profession in general on questions of health, the possibilities of medicine, and the course of dying. Yet the medical profession in no sense holds the important answers to living, dying, and death. We should not in general turn to doctors to tell us the meaning of living, dying, and death. Their education does not teach them those answers. Indeed, in the worst case, their education leads them away from those answers even as their education leads them toward greater technical expertise. Medicine offers a panacea more so than a profound reflection on death. Medicine, for all its enormous good, helps us to look *away* from death in avoidance more so than face death as death ultimately demands. Medicine does not help us reckon a life.

Chapters below, including the chapter on philosophy but especially the chapter on religion, address deeper rationales for medical decision making than simply what medicine makes or does not make available to us, with what affect, and at what cost. Look closely and carefully at medical decisions approaching death, whether you are helping a family member in that process or navigating it yourself. Study and weigh the options. Decide wisely on clear and accurate medical information. Do your medical research. Yet before you get to that point, lay a deeper foundation for making wise medical decisions. Discover the truth about life, dying, and death, and then draw from that truth the rationales that enable you to face death on your discerning terms rather than medicine's terms. Medicine's terms are not a suitable substitute for you to know who you are and what you are about as you or a loved one navigate the shoals of dying to reach the shore of death.

~

He was in the prime of life, just recently engaged to marry, and just finishing graduate school to help transition from one professional career to another, when the diagnosis of an inoperable, malignant, and swiftly spreading brain tumor came. The medical team offered him no hope of any treatment or recovery, nothing at all, not even something dangerously experimental. Thus, he had to decide, what should he do with his last month or two? After sharing his fatal dilemma with his fiancé and professors, he decided simply to stay his current course. He had loved and embraced this part of his life, especially its rediscovery of relationship and learning, no matter what the next stage held, or even if his life held no next stage. So, he, his fiancé, and friends planned a swift wedding at the graduate school. He would stand at the makeshift altar, still just able to do so under his own power, watching his lovely bride walk to him down the aisle. He would continue with his classes as much and for as long as he was able. He and his new bride would live as happily and as fully as his last few days permitted. A month later, friends and family held his memorial in the same room as they had celebrated his wedding.

3

Death and Consciousness

My heart is in anguish within me; the terrors of death have fallen on me.

Psalm 55:4.

Consciousness is clearly an important aspect of being alive, particularly alive *as a human*. Human consciousness is, so far as we know, the universe's single most-consequential event, condition, or attribute, whatever one would properly call it. That we can even examine, consciously, deliberately, thoughtfully, the universe in which we live is an extraordinary capacity, again, the most extraordinary of situations that a universe could sustain. As suggested briefly above, many argue that a person is not even alive unless capable of consciousness. The brain-death standard plays into that assertion, although brain death is a much lower standard for the life-death divide than is consciousness. Those in persistent vegetative states who display no capacity for consciousness are not brain dead. Their hearts beat, they breathe, they sleep and wake, and they respond reflexively to stimuli, not to mention that their brains show abundant waves. In fact, some in persistent vegetative states recover full consciousness. So, consciousness is different than brain death and thus not necessarily critical to life, at least in attempting to define death by traditional or widely accepted standards.

When considering the questions about life and death that persons in vegetative states raise, without apparent consciousness, one has for a moment to realize how poor medicine has been in diagnosing the vegetative. Legal theorist Elizabeth Price Foley, in her book *The Law of Life and Death*, describes three recent studies finding thirty-seven-percent, forty-one-percent, and forty-three-percent error rates in those diagnoses. Research teams trained to observe response commands and purposeful tracking found that less-skilled and more-hurried clinicians were missing patient signals, ones that family members sitting patiently at bedside had sometimes been able to pick up. Many of the misdiagnoses were of blind patients who could not give visual signals but were able to respond to verbal cues, pressing a buzzer to spell out words as the researcher recited the alphabet. Medicine does now recognize a minimally conscious state somewhere between full consciousness and complete vegetative state. Some medical researchers also now believe that the brain may over a longer period be able to regrow damaged nerve connections, known as *axonal regrowth,* as already documented experimentally in monkeys. One extraordinary human case involved recovery of consciousness and speech after a period of nearly two decades in a presumed vegetative state.

Foley recounts another extraordinary case of recovered consciousness after official declarations of permanent vegetative state warranting removal of life support. In that case, medical and state officials sought a court order to remove life support for an eleven-year-old girl whose stepfather had beaten her into a presumed permanent vegetative state just nine days earlier. The stepfather, though, appealed the trial court's grant of the order to remove life support, concerned as he properly was that the abuse charges would become *murder* charges. The stepfather lost the appeal, but the girl miraculously showed signs of consciousness before the medical-care providers could pull her literal and figurative plug. She recovered enough to give authorities statements against her stepfather, whom authorities then convicted of the beating but, the girl still quite alive and further recovering, *not* of murder. Foley recounts other examples of extraordinary recoveries from vegetative states.

Foley also foresees greater use of functional brain imaging to make more-accurate diagnoses of what may truly be going on within the brains of patients diagnosed in permanent vegetative states. As brain-imaging technology continues to improve, and imaging technology grows more widely available, one would think that clinicians would welcome its use in diagnosing the consciousness, life, and death of vegetative-like patients. Yet Foley reports strong resistance to that use. One might, for instance, ask questions of vegetative-appearing patients such as whether they are conscious and in pain, and then use functional imaging to discern their responses and treat them accordingly. Neuro-ethics theorists, though, resist such imaging use because the patient, though cognitively aware and even capable of some form of communication through imaging, would not have the requisite *phenomenal* consciousness that persons recognize and prefer. Some of those theorists have even advocated for euthanasia of the minimally cognitively aware, essentially to put them out of their presumed misery at being able only to minimally think, whether able, now or in the future, to communicate through brain imaging. Nothing, one senses, comes easy in this question of the relationship of consciousness to life and death.

Oddly, reports also arise of persons declared brain dead who are yet conscious, not just *capable* of consciousness, but *conscious*. Legal theorist Foley describes the experience of a twenty-one-year-old man who suffered a brain injury in an accident. The man heard the hospital's doctors declare him brain dead, based on both clinical and diagnostic tests, but could not alert the doctors to his consciousness as they began preparing him for organ donation. In an incredible fortuity, two of the man's cousins, both nurses, showed the attending nurse that he was still responding physically to induced pain. The attending nurse attributed the man's motions to reflex until he jerked his hand across his body away from their pinch. Harvesting preparations promptly stopped, and the man made a slow but substantial recovery. These events of the misdiagnosis of brain death are rare, likely exceedingly rare, but they do happen. Foley makes the point that we must distinguish carefully between judgments that a person is dead and judgments that a person would not want to go on living but would rather die with dignity in their disabled or vegetative state.

Still more oddly, some persistently vegetative patients may even have never fully lost consciousness while in their frozen states. Science journalist Dick Teresi in *The Undead* reports on the first celebrated case of discovering the so-called locked-in patient, in that instance a young woman in a persistent vegetative state who, PET scan revealed, had full brain function, so much as to recognize family photographs and perceive events, even if her complete physical disability kept her from communicating. That person, though still severely physically disabled while possessed of perfect cognitive function, now communicates freely with a letter board and emails, and enjoys the cinema. The explanation of these remarkable states of living while appearing mostly dead lies in that consciousness involves higher cortical function, located in anatomically higher parts of the brain. Medicine has now well documented the condition of some patients, typically after severe stroke, whose loss of lower cortical function (brain-stem function) causes a complete loss of control of any part of the body, even face and eyes. These patients look dead in that they are unable to respond to any stimuli, other than that intensive care and life support can sustain them. Yet they have full cognitive function.

We know of their awareness and consciousness because some have recovered, even after a decade of life support, to describe their anger, confusion, and depression that their caretakers had treated them so indecently, in the sense of having kept them alive but not treated them as living. They see, feel, and hear stimuli, including pain, but cannot react or in any way communicate until, just maybe, the bright lights of a PET scan or some cocktail of stimulating drugs or some other mysterious turn makes them gradually or even suddenly able to speak intelligibly, both questioning the cause of their captive state and describing their horrific experience. Yikes. Most of us would consider the locked-in state to be living, even if desperately so, especially if any prospect for recovery remained, as it did for several locked-in patients who in fact recovered. Advocates exist, yet, for the harvesting of organs from those brain-alive but in persistent vegetative states.

Here, Foley, in *The Law of Life and Death*, notices the outright efforts of some to do away with the dead-donor rule to harvest organs from the living. While society rightly refuses to harvest organs from the living but disabled, degenerated, or demented, a different set of circumstances arises in the case of anencephalic infants who are born without the physiological brain structure to support consciousness. These infants have only lower brain function, just enough to live and breathe at birth, even though they uniformly die at or very shortly after birth. They not only never gain consciousness but are unable to do so for lack of higher brain structure, no less higher brain function. Parents of some of these infants have authorized organ transplants. Yet a year-long experimental protocol failed in trying to remove life support long enough to declare the newborn dead, while preserving the organs for transplant. So, the American Medical Association proposed to allow organ transplants from the living newborns, only later to withdraw its proposal in the face of public outcry. Fortunately, the incidence of anencephaly then fell, following new early pregnancy regimens. Improved transplantation techniques also reduced the demand for newborns' organs.

Foley also questions the premise that the higher brain is the locus of consciousness. Apparently, the lower brain or brain stem interacts in complex fashion with other brain structures, in ways that science and medicine little understand. The lower brain may have a lot to do with the emotions and even with consciousness, more so than advocates for a higher-brain-death standard admit. Consciousness, cognition, and higher-order thinking may to degrees originate in, find support from, be influenced by, and thus co-exist within the brain stem and other brain regions. The *person* or *identity* may lie as much in the brain stem and its activity, emotions, and influences as in other structures of the brain, questioning not only the higher-brain-death standard but even the nebulous concept of *consciousness*. Where, after all, does a person's character lie, in the person's conscious thought, deep emotions, or instant inclinations, or even in the heart? Foley raises the possibility, for which one finds scant law, that society should permit a person not only to die as they choose but also to live as they choose by defining their own terms of death, whether consciousness, higher brain, lower brain, cardiopulmonary, or rigor mortis. Why should law exclusively define our life and death? Or to put the question another way, why shouldn't law preserve for us an individual right to define when we are dead?

Plainly, the question of consciousness thus becomes an important one for understanding death, even if consciousness is probably not necessary to live and may, frighteningly for the locked-in patient, not be quite sufficient to appear to be living. The attribute and criterion *consciousness*, though, raises the possibility that we are mental beings, or soul beings, or spiritual beings, more so than, or even independently from, our material, biological being. The question of consciousness and the role it plays in defining life and death forces thinkers, like the philosophy lecturer Belshaw in his book *Annihilation*, to distinguish the *person* from the *human being*, the sense of who we are when conscious, from the biological organism in which our consciousness habitually resides. Consciousness is obviously the strong sense of who we are, critical to the full identity of the person whose life one considers, whether the one doing the consideration is the conscious person or is others, such as family and friends, with whom the person interacts. Death, though, a biological phenomenon, clearly differs from consciousness.

Near-death experiences help in different ways to illustrate consciousness's significance to dying, whether to experiencing death itself or not. The problem with near-death experiences is that the many persons who report them, in such numbers and with such reliability as to convince many firm skeptics that the experiences do exist, is that the reporters did not die, at least not irreversibly, that single criterion being a key part of most working definitions of death. Their examiners may have declared them dead. They may in respects have been momentarily, clinically, the equivalent of a dead person, but whatever or wherever they were, they returned to themselves to report their experiences. As science journalist Teresi reports in *The Undead*, government and public-university psychiatrists and psychologists have documented and studied the many near-death or through-death experiences, which go something like the following. A trauma or episode occurs that leads medical-care providers to believe the person to be dead, perhaps even declaring them dead. The person, though, remains fully conscious, aware somehow of the sight, sound, and other senses of the death experience, often outside of the body or in a different kind of body, led down tunnel or toward light by or to other transformed relatives or beings, only at the last moment instructed back to their resuscitating body.

What makes these experiences, in the millions according to some polling, notable is that some instances have occurred under clinical circumstances appearing to make it difficult to accept that they are only dreams or distorted consciousness. Teresi reports one cardiologist's study, published in one of the world's most-reputable medical journals, of hundreds of resuscitated cardiac-arrest victims, about one-fifth of whom recounted near-death experiences despite the cessation of cardiac function, blood flow, and observable brain waves. While the published data, if not all its author's conclusions, largely held up under scrutiny, and some neuropsychiatric experts admitted that the study created a scientific puzzle, others disagreed that the study and similar reports meant that consciousness could exist apart from the living brain of the whole organism, which is the controversial conclusion some would draw. Extraordinary cases sharpen the interpretive disagreement. In one instance, a woman recounted details of her own brain surgery (along with details of the transporting beings of light) in which physicians had shut down her heart, lungs, and brain in hypothermic cardiac arrest, eliminating even reflex response of her closed eyes, plugging her ears, and flat-lining her brain waves. She still thought, saw, heard, and experienced her surgery's events, along with details of her heavenly transport. Teresi reports that many persons undergoing near-death experiences enjoy long-lasting, positive changes in their lives. Dying, apparently, may not always be a precise moment but instead for some a journey that leaves the feeling of possible sharp and miraculous reverse.

Increases in near-death experiences, and increased interest in them and reporting of them, are understandably modern phenomena. In the past, dying persons were usually very soon dead. Widespread and effective short-term resuscitation techniques are modern inventions. Cardiologist and medical professor Haider

Warraich, in his book *Modern Death*, reports that the key integration of core cardiopulmonary resuscitation techniques occurred only in 1960. Ventilation, defibrillation, and chest compression were developing techniques long before then, but their combination in precise, readily achievable CPR protocol revolutionized and standardized resuscitation practices. Promptly after this defining moment in modern medicine, huge numbers of healthcare workers received proper CPR training, even as emergency-response systems added trained paramedics to ambulances, communities implemented the new 911 response system, and the new Medicare law made such services far more widely available. Many more began to survive cardiac arrest in near-death experiences.

The attribute consciousness, and the *personhood* concept that often accompanies it, do raise the question of human value. What are we worth, either alive or dead? Again, the philosophy lecturer Belshaw makes some revealing and helpful assertions. The reasonable commitment that we should not treat the living as if they were dead suggests that the living have greater value to us. Yet we also rightly respect the memory of, and thus in some sense value, the dead. Indeed, society may judge a greater offense speaking ill of the dead than of the living. The dead cannot defend themselves. And society does in special cases treat the living as if dead, in some cases withholding nutrition and hydration from the comatose until they die, and in other cases removing life support from the living-but-presumed-brain-dead while preparing to harvest their organs. Oddly, in the latter case, the medical team harvesting the organs first briefly removes the life support, long enough to declare the patient dead, then promptly restores the life support and swiftly increases the medical regimen and attention for the successful harvest, treating the dead better, or at least more so, than the living. In these cases, the most-sophisticated medical care comes *after* death, in some cases with the patient, family, or other authority having decided not to provide more care before death.

As previously mentioned, advocates for the higher irreversible-loss-of-consciousness standard for death, one that would promote better medical care for the presumed-dead unconscious to preserve and harvest their healthy organs, than for the conscious but terminally ill who should soon be dying, tend to reach their position by rejecting that humans have any capacity for transcendence. Chau and Herring in their chapter *The Meaning of Death* take the argument one step further, arguing that we should reject even the concept of consciousness, which they maintain is only an illusion. Their view is that neuropsychology and brain imaging have proven that our thinking, recognition, emotions, and even mental disorders are only anatomical, physiological, chemical, or electrical changes in our brain state. In their view, we have no mind, certainly no mind-body duality. Their view, one that they say is the scientific view, is that we are only a *physiological machine*. And given that conclusion, they argue that those who retain the will and capacity should adopt for the rest of us a *more mechanistic* definition of death. That position could mean defining the mentally ill, diseased, or unproductive disabled *as dead*. Even if one does not go that far and instead retains a consciousness standard for death, Chau and Herring acknowledge that one could potentially classify the very mentally ill as dead because not conscious. Plainly, removing transcendence from the human equation leaves little ethical bound. One wonders whether such advocates feel their argument's chill, even if they profess no mind for comprehending it.

The question of human value that personhood and consciousness tend to implicate also raises the issue of whether death is generally or uniformly bad, and if either or both, then how bad. Don't be too surprised: one increasingly popular modern secular view, readily associated with the ancient Greek philosopher Epicurus who clearly so stated in one of his few surviving writings, is that death is never bad for the person who dies. Death can certainly be bad for dependent survivors who lose the decedent's love, society, and support. Epicurus's point was that the person who dies is no longer conscious and thus no longer around to experience death's loss. The response of many including philosophy lecturer Belshaw is that conceptually, at least, one can reasonably say that the decedent has a loss as extensive as the good that the decedent would have enjoyed during the life that the decedent would have lived but for the death. You can see that the response presumes that a bad death is a premature death, death that occurs before natural death. To die in the prime of a good life is great loss, while to die at the end of a good or bad life is less loss or none, although just how one measures the loss or how much confidence one can have in the conclusion are very much open to question. Maybe the person who dies in the prime of a good life was about to become very unhappy or die soon of other, natural causes.

Consider here the question of martyrdom. For better or worse, some have used their consciousness, their life and conscious deliberation, to die for a cause. For example, religions professor Talat Halman, in his chapter *Death Is Its Own Conquest* in the book *Unequal Before Death*, writes how some adherents construe the Quran to authorize not suicide but deliberate death, indeed as a hallmark terrorist battle tactic of Islamic State, Al Qaeda, and Palestinian extremists. To those extremists, the willingness, indeed eagerness to die to promote the faith is a heroic act worthy both of gaining Allah's paradise and a celebrated legacy in martyrdom. Glorifying suicide bombers in posters, film, ceremony, and rallies is also a political strategy, one that not only religious officials but also educators, artists, media, and political leaders promote, Halman gives the example, for Palestinian independence. Women and teenagers wearing explosive suicide belts do not, in that view, face a death sentence but instead anticipate a hero's celebration and a ticket to Allah's heaven.

Martyrs, though, need not in other contexts kill themselves and as many innocent others as possible to receive a hero's celebration. The cause need not be religious or political conquest but instead may be religious or other liberty, and peace. We do not know the fate of the unidentified Tank Man, as we now call him, who stood in front of a column of advancing tanks in Beijing's Tiananmen Square, as the Chinese military suppressed protests, although his actions easily qualify as heroic, as he shifted quietly back and forth to block the advancing and maneuvering tanks. Biblical martyrs who stood peacefully for the faith include Zebedee's son James, Jesus's brother James, and Stephen. Early Christian tradition adds the apostles Peter and Paul. The Age of Martyrdom added Polycarp, Justin Martyr, Perpetua and Felicity, Ptolemaeus and Lucius, Euphemia, Cyprian, and many celebrated others. The Middle Ages added Valentine, Ludmila, Thomas Becket, Jerome, Joan of Arc, and many others. The

Reformation added Thomas More, William Tyndale, Anne Askew, Thomas Cranmer, and Margaret Ball, and many others. Modern Christian martyrs are also countless. *Consciousness* can lead to *conscience* and, in a violent and corrupt world, a martyr's peace-loving and instructive death.

Perhaps consciousness's problem, then, is not so much death but time, as Arthur Schopenhauer wrote in *On the Vanity of Existence*. Death is only problematic because of time's march toward it. If instead time stood still, and we could live eternally in each moment or any moment, then death would not darken or lighten our future. Yet time certainly doesn't stand still, not for us at least. Schopenhauer shows that presuming that death means eternal loss of consciousness and end of one's self, casts a nihilistic shadow over life. All striving then becomes vanity, pointless chasing after things that mean nothing to others and little or nothing to one's self because of death's end. Death, in the nihilist's view, destroys all possibility of meaningful life, unless one takes a tiny bit of self-fulfillment, pursuing pleasurably whatever talents one finds within one's self, as life's only measure. Consciousness, in that view, is simply to dwell on the pleasure, to recognize that one has drawn on one's talents for whatever conscious experience those talents entail. Live being aware that one enjoys certain aspects of life, the view holds, for that introspection is all that life offers. Life is, the view again holds, a closed loop, consciousness looking in on its own experience, isolated and ultimately pointless other than the fact of the closed loop.

Consciousness, though, holds another possibility beyond looking in on itself, as the experience of the martyrs suggests. The point to draw from consciousness is not that life is in consciousness itself, as to some degree the nihilist must conclude. Rather, consciousness offers a broader purpose relating to death. Consciousness reminds us that we may *use* consciousness to determine how one faces death. Consciousness gives us the capacity to look beyond ourselves, to turn outward rather than inward, to connect to the timeless and true. Consciousness gives us the means to discover what history has offered us not just in life but even as to death. With consciousness, we can examine the record of history to choose a course that lends the greatest possible meaning to death. Consciousness ultimately gives us the prospect for facing and overcoming death, even for *defeating* death if its defeat is possible. One does not stumble into truth and its possibilities, or at least very few likely do. Consciousness gives us the means to do more than stumble through life into death. When we deploy consciousness as it invites and even begs us to do, consciousness gives us control not only over who we are and what we do but also how we encounter death.

One sees the value of consciousness, of deliberation and contemplation over the fact and approach of death, in the extraordinary attention and care that we give, or should give, to the dying. The anthology *Making Sense of Bereavement* collects stories of the rewards and challenges of that care. One recounts a mother's gradual, Alzheimer's induced journey away from her loving daughter, into a life-of-the-nursing-home-party fantasy that turned the daughter into an imagined mother. Another recounts a son's loving struggle to respect his dying, dependent father's desired and entitled independence. Another recounts a daughter's effort to help her mother and father through a harrowing maze of medical incompetency and professional insolence, to their deaths. Another explores the different role that friends and neighbors take, different from family members and professionals, in caring for the dying. Others tell the critical roles and tender experiences of hospital porters, social workers, and chaplains, in tending to the dead and dying. In each of these stories, and other stories describing the sacrificial suffering of caregivers, one sees how intimate and rich the process of dying can be for the fully conscious.

The significance of consciousness to living, dying, and death often plays out around the death bed. For better or worse, most of us die in bed, and not necessarily *asleep* in bed but rather in a sort of drama around the death bed. Family members and caretakers alternate watching over the death bed, while family members and lawyers record the last wishes, and ministers note the last words, of the dying. Historian Philippe Aries in his book *The Hour of Our Death* notes, though, how over time the scene of the death bed has changed. The death bed is no longer routinely in the home but instead more often in the nursing home or hospital. Material care through technological means has replaced spiritual and emotional care through human relationship. While last rites and confessions, including forgiveness of wrongdoers and absolution for wrongs, were once the central drama around the death bed, the social and spiritual drama is now instead a medical ordeal. Even in our last moments, technology has changed us. The great moral struggle to make sense of a lifetime of good and bad, pain and pleasure, love and hate, and the warring of angels and demons over the dying one's soul, has now become a great material struggle to squeeze out a few more days and weeks, or if not that, then to make of death a painless passage into nothingness. In that shift, a conscious death, one that reflects on the course and significance of one's life, reflection that was once critical, seems much less important. Better do that reflection now before falling into the medical course's grip.

Indeed, Aries charts at length, through the Middle Ages and Renaissance into modernity, death's desanctification and, as he calls it, *dethronement.* If death involved judgment, then it must fully engage the dying one's consciousness and conscience. If the state of the dying one's soul had eternal implications, then conscious deliberation must continually inform that soul until consciousness is no longer able. One must have died a good death, running the race to its end, with death edifying the runner at every step. Death above all entailed sobriety. The hour of death was significant, indeed critical, as demons tried to wrest renunciation from the saved and sanctified soul. Yet if, in Renaissance's new secular ideology, death did not in any sense involve the soul because we are soulless animals, biological machines that our genes direct, then death makes no difference. We may then die as libertines, in obstinate slavery to our mortality, freed of the liberty of the eternal. Illness to the libertine is not a warning for reform, a call to conversion, but instead an opportunity to mock a supposedly illusory God while committing the soul to the devil. To die as an animal, without reflection on one's life, dying, and death, would then be better, for animals we are, in the modern secular spirit. The hour of death has no special meaning, then. An art of living pleasurably replaces the art of living rightly to die well.

Aries also records how, as the secular age dethroned death as judge, it simultaneously exalted death within our new self-encrypted narcissism. While in the sacred age, death came from the outside, trying in its hardship and fear to steal one's soul, in the secular age life itself becomes a celebration of the dead and macabre, life corrupted by its vanity. Death in the secular age becomes a haven at the heart of culture and consciousness, rather than an enemy and warning. Death then mocks pleasure, making suspect the full span of life from birth to death. Whereas hope had once leavened the natural melancholy that accompanies death reflections, the secular age, by removing hope, made consciousness all melancholy. One could no longer enjoy pleasures. And so, while on the one hand we pursue pleasure as the only meaning, and then grovel in it having given it such inappropriate ultimate place, on the other hand we must reject pleasure, too, as meaningless, adopting an asceticism not borne of faith but of despair because all is vanity.

History has given us the choice instead to pursue a relationship that offers to overcome our death. Consciousness, deliberation over the one who made that offer, is the means through which we pursue that relationship. One cannot love without knowledge of the other for whom one cares and whom one pursues. Consciousness makes love possible. As later chapters further explore, consciousness gives us the capacity for knowledge of the one on whom our relationship must fix to face and overcome death. Consciousness thus has a purpose so essential and wonderful as to imbue life with all that it might ever hold. Yes, we should be conscious of the experience of life including the blessing that it holds. Yet we should not stop short with contemplating those experiences as we enjoy them, as if the experiences were the closed-loop end of life. We instead benefit most, and those around us benefit most, when we turn the reflection outward beyond the gifts to the giver of those gifts who offers so much more than those gifts by offering himself.

~

He had just left his court internship, walking past a parking structure next to his law school, when a *thump* sound made him notice what he at first thought was a bag of trash just ahead of him fallen to the sidewalk. He looked up, thinking that someone had thrown the bag off the top of the parking structure. But then, the bag moved and moaned, and he realized that the object was a woman who had just jumped or fallen from the five-story structure. Frightened and revolted, he nonetheless approached her, put down his briefcase, and, while shouting to passersby to call 911, in his business suit kneeled on the sidewalk and bent over her to listen to her mumbling. She was scared, she said, and in pain, and sorry. She wanted her sister and family to know that she loved them. And she, a poor, homeless, disheveled, desperate, and dying black woman, wanted this young white male intern so full of hope and promise to pray for her. He bent further over her and prayed quietly, reassuringly, and then passionately and tearfully, as a crowd gathered around them and she said her last words, fell into silence, and died. No one knew of the young intern's courageous compassion until a month later, when the law school held a memorial for the homeless woman who had frequented the mission next door, her family attended, and the young intern stepped forward to share with the family his prayer and the dying woman's comforted last words.

4

Death and Art

In my Father's house are many rooms; if it were not so, I would have told you. I am going there to prepare a place for you. And if I go and prepare a place for you, I will come back and take you to be with me that you also may be where I am.

John 14:1-3.

Art fundamentally arises out of death, writes art curator and lecturer Chris Townsend in his book *Art and Death*. Townsend begins with German philosopher Martin Heidegger's construct, described in greater detail in the chapter below on death and philosophy, that our being arises out of our willingness to comprehend our own coming death. Townsend, though, observes that we cannot fully experience our own death but instead only the death of others. Death, as we think of it, thus lies not within our own experience but only within our conjecture as to the experiences of others. Death is in that sense *other regarding*, a pointing outward from ourselves to others. In that death-induced projection of our interest and concern, from ourselves outward to others, lies not only the source of ethics and politics but also the source of art and culture. Every artistic effort, whether to paint, film, sing, or dance, is to construct or reconstruct the ethical, political, social, and historical relationship to the other. And so, the earliest cave paintings are of hunters dying on the horns of their powerful prey, and hunters who are dead, painted not by the dying hunter but by the living hunter to make sense of facing death.

Yet Townsend further argues that no one, not even the artist, truly makes sense of death. Crediting the writing of philosopher Jacques Derrida, Townsend discerns that death, more so than anything other than God, lies beyond definable experience. Because for lack of direct, personal experience we cannot make a determinate sign, symbol, or object out of death, leaving death only as an indefinable limit, death demands and effectuates knowledge and meaning rather than submitting to knowledge and meaning. Death produces art and culture rather than being its subject and object. Art and culture arise out of death, whether in embrace or avoidance. Neither art nor culture can define death, ensuring that we approach death only indirectly because of its experiential impossibility. Art arises in its deepest form, beyond entertainment or commodity, only because the death of the portrait subject and artist, sooner or later, enlivens it. Death is the gift that marries responsibility to faith, fostering through art and culture a risk-all form of involvement with one another that exceeds competence and knowledge. History begins at precisely that point where art and culture arise in involvement with death.

If you have any doubt of the power of death over art, then consider that Townsend credits art's Western tradition to continual reinterpretations of the death of the God-man Christ by slow asphyxiation, nailed hand and foot, and spear thrust confirming his death. As Townsend's analysis suggests, artists throughout the ages have depicted a full range of traditional, sensitive, frightening, absurd, and challenging views of dying and death. Artistic depictions of dying and death have helped many face death, for instance to see and accept that death will come, of which some of us need reminder. One has only to walk past a church fresco of the crucified Christ or past the town founder's statue, or to drive by the obelisks and vaults of the cemetery, or to watch the war, terror, and disaster images on the news, or flick through them on social media on our smartphones. Artistic, literary, and media images give us daily, even hour-by-hour reminders of our mortality, not just in memorial statues and passion paintings but also in televised images of mass graves, airplane crashes, and archaeological discovery of ancient human bones. Visual images of dying, death, and the disposal of remains are so frequent that their reminders lurk just beneath our consciousness, like the dark clouds on the distant horizon.

The anthology *Making Sense of Death, Dying and Bereavement* opens with a collection of those visual images. An exquisite woodcut has a woman and boy visiting a man sunken low in his hospital bed, the woman sitting with bowed head on the foot of the bed with the little boy standing close by her as if to take shelter in her health against fear of the man's demise. A similar deathbed-scene etching by nineteenth-century Austrian illustrator Alfred Kubin shows two healthy visitors peering intently at the dying ward propped uncomfortably up in the deathbed. Photographs depict the bright or solemn clothes that old Croatian women have set aside in advance for their burial. A dramatic Henry Wallis painting of the dead seventeen-year-old Romantic English poet Thomas Chatterton stands next to post-mortem photographs showing the genuinely dead as if peacefully asleep. Photographs capture roadside memorials, both official and unofficial. Image after image, each tells a different story of death. Even a death certificate leaves its artistic impression, its subtly symmetrical boxes and lines of hand-scripted information assembled carefully beneath a heralding coat of arms and grave title, plainly to make order out of chaos and pronouncement out of what too often passes with bare notice.

Other artistic images of death are more intentional. Titian's early Renaissance painting *The Three Ages of Man*, variously dated to 1512 to 1515, is a premier example of the breadth with which art can treat the subject of life and death while playfully challenging the viewer. Titian's work in the foreground depicts mature lovers about to embrace, in the middle ground sleeping infants over which Cupid watches, and in the background a pensive, aged St. Jerome contemplating two skulls, perhaps of former lovers, with a church on the far hill in the background. One sees in the painting the full course of life from conception to end, with death looming only implicitly in the darkening sky. Similarly, Gustav Klimt in his 1916 painting *Death and Life* shows the club-bearing, skulled figure of death peering ominously into a bright womb of hugging and huddling infant-to-aged figures who close their eyes and turn away from death's threat. Once again, Klimt captures the full course of life, from conception to end, although here death stands in explicit eagerness, as if waiting to seize life.

Painters depict not only looming death but the dead themselves. Jacques-Louis David's 1793 *The Death of Marat* captured his dead friend, a radical journalist whose murderer held him responsible for the French Revolution's violence, dead in his bath but still gracefully holding his pen and correspondence, head tipped back as if in blissful fulfillment. The murder weapon, a blood-stained, white-handled knife, lies just below the dead figure who drapes gently over the edge of his coffin bath. Cezanne in 1868 and 1869 painted *Preparation for the Funeral* depicting the lifelessly plastic corpse drawing the earnest but similarly lifeless mortician in, while a woman turns away in disgust to the living world that she plainly prefers. Pablo Picasso in 1901's *Death of Casagemas* likewise depicted his dead friend, although less dramatically, showing only the figure's flame-lit head, in blue hues anticipating Picasso's own blue period. Vincent Van Gogh in 1885 to 1886 painted a skull clenching a burning cigarette in its teeth, an image that viewers today would interpret as an anti-smoking campaign but that would have meant something very different to viewers then. The painting may have evoked that the viewer should realize the viewer's mortality even while engaging in the mundane pleasures and diversions of the day. Edvard Munch, best known for his four compositions popularly named *The Scream*, in his 1895 painting *By the Deathbed* turned the focus from the dead figure, barely shown at all under white bed sheets, to the grief-stricken bedside mourners, one of whom looks not at the dead figure but back at the viewer as if to say *you're next*.

Painters have simultaneously shocked, guided, and consoled their works' viewers about death. Matthias Grunewald painted the Isenheim altarpiece in the early 1500's to depict the crucified Christ in savagely brutalized form, covered with sores like those of which locals were then dying horrible, gangrenous deaths. Open the altarpiece's panels, though, and one sees a resplendently resurrected Christ. Similarly, fifteenth-century German painter Memling in

Triptych of Earthly Vanity and Divine Salvation placed a healthy figure vainly admiring herself in a mirror between a ghastly figure of death and an equally frightening panel showing a struggle to raise a figure from hell. Coming out of two near-fatal illnesses, Francisco de Goya between 1819 and 1823 painted a series known as his *black paintings*, the darkest of which may well be *Saturn Devouring His Son*, in which the voracious god consumes the bloodied top half of a clearly human figure. Some of these paintings depict clear meanings, while others leave the viewer to ponder just what to draw.

American writer/critic Edgar Allan Poe's short story *The Premature Burial* and Belgian painter Antoine Wiertz's work *The Hasty Burial* give form to the fear of a declaration of death while one still lives. Wiertz's painting shows the living but purportedly deceased figure struggling to shove open the lid of his plain wooden casket, stacked with other caskets outside the tomb. Poe's work told the first-person story of a protagonist who, prone to falling into death-like trances, was so fearful of living burial as not to leave his own home. Of course, the story ends with the figure waking in confined pitch blackness. Wiertz's painting and Poe's story were both 1850 works, at a time when reports were growing of persons struggling successfully to alert their pall bearers that they were not yet dead and exhumation of caskets showing that the deceased had lived long enough to struggle unsuccessfully to get out of the casket. Ancient and traditional practices once accounted in different ways for the possibility that the presumed dead might still be living or might arise after death. Medical and embalming practices have largely ended those practices, at least in America. Today, the dead are usually dead.

Photographers have contributed their own talents to visual studies of death. Francesca Woodman committed suicide leaping out of a window at age twenty-two but not before taking and exhibiting a series of black-and-white interior scenes depicting her own ghostly figure in odd positions, altered, smudged, or fading out in eerily beautiful, wraith-like form. Woodman's suicide haunts the otherworldly images, which have moved so many as to hang in the Guggenheim Museum. Photographs of the dead enjoyed brief popularity, as a new form of *memento mori*, or remembrance of the dead, in the mid 1800's around photography's birth. Photographs of the living were then so rare and expensive as to make the figure's death a cause and excuse for the expenditure. Some photographs posed the living around the dead, blurring the living slightly because of their small movements made during the long exposures, while capturing the dead in perfect image. Some photographers painted eyes on the images of the dead to make their appearance more lifelike. As photography became less expensive, and photographs of the living became common, families lost cause to photograph their dead.

American photographer Peter Hujar juxtaposed black-and-white photographs of famous living artists against photographs of the very-long dead in his 1976 book *Portraits in Life and Death*. Hujar had explored Palermo, Italy's catacombs, taking eerie, chilling, and yet somehow poignant images of the skeletons and mummified remains propped here and there in their corners, coffins, and crude wood-and-stone sarcophagi. The corpse photographs' artistic sensitivity, each image lit, angled, and composed with a master's skill, leavens only slightly Hujar's palpable offense in stealing the images from the dead. His placing the corpse images next to images of his famous writer, artist, film director, and actor friends, make the living appear to reflect on their mortality, as writer and subject Susan Sontag discerns in the book's introduction. Photographs, Sontag writes, instantly turn the present into permanent past, both venerating and cheapening the subject by making today's banal into tomorrow's legacy. Photography makes the mortal immortal while making a totem of mortality, every photograph of the living instantly a record of soon-to-be death. Photographers, Sontag discerned, are the *recording angels* of death, a status that Hujar both captured and mocked in his contrasted portraits of living and dead, both exorcising and succumbing to morbidity.

Sontag's insights on Hujar's photograph indeed show that writers are most readily able to state expressly their views on and experiences of living, dying, and death. Life, Shakespeare famously wrote in the *Tragedy of Macbeth,* is but a *tale told by an idiot, full of sound and fury, signifying nothing.* Novelist/philosopher Jean-Paul Sartre, in his first and, he felt, best novel *Nausea,* had his narrator assert that he had simply *appeared by chance* to exist *like a stone*, so that he felt nothing other than an *inconsequential buzzing* in that life held *nothing, nothing, absolutely no reason for existing*. Others find themselves unable to reach any such answer about life's meaning or meaninglessness, like atheist philosopher Bertrand Russell who ended his life at age 95 writing in his *Last Essay* that no answer is possible to whether he served any purpose or instead lived a life of futility because one doesn't know the future. Russell's hope, then, was to let loose the *artist imprisoned in each one of us* who would then *spread joy everywhere*, as philosophy professor John Messerly quotes in his book *The Meaning of Life*. Perhaps so, although one doesn't need to be clueless about the future to release one's artist for spreading joy. Clues for the future abound for those who wish to pursue them, artists embracing those clues having created glorious imagery.

Many have written artistically, emotionally, sensitively, and passionately about bereavement and death, in painfully evocative memoirs. Joan Didion's *The Year of Magical Thinking*, Joyce Carol Oates's *A Widow's Story*, and C. S. Lewis's *A Grief Observed* are prominent examples among them. Writing the bereavement memoir is therapy. Writing is a premier act of consciousness, constantly reflective of thought, while constantly recording and memorializing that reflection. Writing thus challenges death, flies in the face of death, denies death, if one is able. *See*, Bertrand Russell could say about my quote of him above, *my art did survive my death; they're still quoting me*. Maria-Jose Blanco, in her chapter *Understanding Death/Writing Bereavement: The Writer's Experience*, in the collected work *The Power of Death: Contemporary Reflection on Death in Western Society*, suggests that writing at least helps to manage grief if not entirely to cure it. She cites Lewis as prime example, trying to proceed with his life after the cancer-wrought death of his beloved wife Joy Gresham, whom he identified only as *H* in his *A Grief Observed*. Suffering, Lewis wrote there, includes knowledge that one suffers, looking at misery's shadow or reflection. Lewis managed to write his way past grief's grip, avoiding the total collapse that grief tantalizingly invited. Didion, for her part also writing of a beloved spouse's passing, wrote her own magical memoir while also reading Lewis's to help her cope.

Fiction and poetry have special power to represent the inevitable challenges of death and dying. The anthology *Making Sense of Death, Dying and Bereavement* excerpts a dozen good examples. Author Mitch Albom in *The Five People You Meet in Heaven* depicts the death and afterlife of an old man whom the death and near death of two young girls had haunted. Author Jacqueline Wilson in the children's book *Vicky Angel* helps young readers face their first encounter with death, in a story of the death of a young friend by motor-vehicle accident. Poet John Keats writes an *Ode to a Nightingale* while poet Dylan Thomas in *Do Not Go Gentle into that Good Night* urges rage against the dying light. Joseph Heller in the war novel *Catch 22* depicts a scene of parents visiting a military hospital, too late to console their dead soldier son, instead consoling a dying soldier as if he was their own son. One discovers in these and similar writings everything from poignancy and sentimentality to the most macabre and disturbing humor.

Literature, so committed to exploring the profound, naturally takes up the subject of dying, most notably in Leo Tolstoy's *The Death of Ivan Ilych*, a familiar and most-frequently cited novella. Literature professor Victor Brombert, in his book *Musings on Mortality*, calls the story deceptively simple. The fictional Ilych, named nondescriptly as if he could have been anyone, was a cultured jurist who spent his life drawing meaningless pride from the trivial, only to discover so in his last days. Death faced him down utterly, inescapably, and not that Ilych could *do* anything about it other than to look more and more at his approaching death. Ilych no longer drew any comfort from his urbane company, all of whom, like Ilych himself, had spent their lives looking away from death rather than letting death draw meaning into their lives. Only the peasant Gerasim, whose rural life had kept him humbly and spiritually close to birth, life, and death, could in his blunt words and kind service provide Ilych any comfort. Although Ilych died with precious little comfort, no legacy, and in utter spiritual void, his realizing the vanity of his life at least opened for him, or more pointedly for the reader rather than the fictional Ilych, a salvific door, one that Tolstoy crafted exquisitely into necessary last-page ambiguity, the author knowing that one turns away from preaching but to the open door. Literature professor Brombert sees in that ending faint allusion to John Donne's sonnet *Death, Be Not Proud*, concluding, *Death shall be no more: Death, though shalt die!*

Readers also know the French philosopher-author Albert Camus, artful depicter of the absurd, for his literary reflections on death. Camus' novel *The Stranger* opens with the narrator relating the death of his mother and closes with the narrator jailed and awaiting execution for that death. His novel *The Plague* depicts a dead city, one without birds and trees, beset by dying rats, as the plague also decimates the city's soulless residents. Camus, though, objected to the existentialist label that some put on him, indeed rejected all ideology, seeing destruction in historical movements like the then-popular Hegelian philosophy. Instead pursuing an elusive transcendentalism, Camus abhorred violence, afforded life supreme value, and took strong, public stances against capital punishment, while also finding precious joy in life. Camus simply let ever-present mortality, hard to ignore through two World Wars the first of which killed his father, and tuberculosis that plagued the author, further imbue his life with its fearful value. Brombert discerns in Camus' writing an important distinction between reflecting on mortality, which can be quite healthy for its recognition that one is alive, and reflection on death, tending toward unhealthy morbidity.

Fyodor Dostoevsky traces a similar trajectory in *The Idiot*, where a character recounts an event like one that occurred in the author's own life, in which a man who faces execution wins reprieve just minutes before his death. Imminent death, though, had focused the man on how he would live if given such a reprieve, treating each moment as an eternity, missing nothing in life. Take nothing for granted, seize all opportunity, and live as if each moment must last for an eternity, the lesson draws. Do not wallow in death but instead draw frequent flickers of imagination from it. Treasure suffering, the real pain of facing physical demise, for these lessons that death can teach. Remember the ghost of Jacob Marley in Charles Dickens' *A Christmas Carol*, who answered Scrooge's terrified question, "What do you want with me?" with the equally terrifying answer, "Much!" In those moments when confronting death, one may see a glimmer of the possibility of transcendent life that death must hold, and then seize and celebrate it, as the great English poet and bishop John

Donne wrote in the poem already referenced. Follow the path the greatest poet John Milton traced in the greatest poem *Paradise Lost* and its companion *Paradise Regained*. Novelist and literary critic John Updike, in his poem *Seven Stanzas at Easter*, repeated the warning to *let us not mock God with metaphor* by *making of the event a parable* that one paints *in the faded credulity of earlier ages*. Instead, *let us walk through the door*, Updike writes. Do not, like English literary critic and poet William Empson wrote, believe instead that one *should be prepared to be blank upon* the meaning and consequences of death.

Authors have explored in the most compelling of ways life and death without the transcendent. Mary Shelley in her 1818 novel *Frankenstein, or the Modern Prometheus*, famously had the title-named doctor collect and stitch together parts of the dead, in which, the Gothic would hold, one still finds animation for life. All that life then took was a sort of galvanism, lightning's bolt, to bring the creature to life. Of course, the creature without a divine creator and with only organic and not supernatural life, is a monster. Shelley's literary accomplishment was to draw together the Gothic and Romantic into a form that later informed the new genre of science fiction. Her conceptual gift was to depict unforgettably the corruption of the purely organic, how if matter possesses an energy capable of forming life, then that life stands without beauty, order, or ethic. Witness the violently and criminally sensual French revolutionary Marquis de Sade, who modeled what the language in dark homage calls *sadism*.

Literature thus helps us wrestle with this question whether we have such a transcendent standard against which, or being against whom, to measure a life, even as we contemplate death. Playwright Arthur Miller in *After the Fall* has his character Quentin see the despair of life without God judging its quality. If no judge is on the bench, then life has no upward path, Quentin reflects. Whether one is brave or smart as a young man, then a good father, and eventually wise or powerful or whatever, presumes justification or condemnation from the judge's bench, a cosmic verdict. Without that inherent sense of continuing judgment, life is merely disaster, an *endless argument with oneself*. Transcendence thus doesn't merely relieve one of a future death but relieves one of present meaninglessness. Standards not only constrain but enliven and inform. Authority imbues the universe not as a tyrant but as a lover, as one making all things beautiful and new.

Even one so accomplished as Leo Tolstoy asked in his *A Confession* whether his life had any meaning *that the inevitable death awaiting me does not destroy*. He wanted to know what would come *of what I am doing today or tomorrow*, what would come *of my whole life*, and whether anything was worth doing. Death clearly calls to the artist's mind what philosophy professor Steven Luper, in the chapter *Life's Meaning* in the *Cambridge Companion*, calls the *achievementist* view of life. This view holds that life's only meaning is achievement of the aims and objectives that you in your liberty pursue. Luper clarifies that *you* do not bear that meaning as much as *your life* bears the meaning of your achievements. Aims are those things, cumulatively, for which we live, not so much moment to moment, as in ensuring a full stomach and sufficient rest, but in their arc and whole. Aims toward achievements give life purpose. Aims also give one's life *identity*, and not just identity like blond hair or green eyes but conative identity, the form that one chooses to have. One can certainly live life to achieve a great end. As Luper points out at his chapter's conclusion, one can even live life to leave an unfinished great end, whether a research project, novel, painting, or great building, that one hopes and expects others will finish.

See, then, that the artist may, in the liberty that art implies, draw meaning from just such aims, purpose, and identity. After all, art is the artist's effective pursuit of creative, unique, and original expression. I know. I grew up in a family of artists, although I hardly counted myself one. My mother was an award-winning and commercially successful potter and a papermaker, photographer, writer, and bookmaker, among a half-dozen other creative roles. My brother is a painter, photographer, custom-furniture maker, and musical-instrument and motorcycle builder, likewise among a half-dozen other creative roles. But my father, appropriately named *Art*, was the one who most embraced and pursued art, which for him included primarily architecture but also drawing, silk-screening, woodworking, and photography, yes, among a half-dozen other creative roles. The evidence of his avid and admirably successful pursuits was everywhere, surrounding him in the homes that he built, with his photographs, prints, plans, and drawings hanging on the walls. He once asked me, at a difficult moment in his life when he needed encouragement, what I thought *of his art*. I wanted to say that although it was obviously abundant and admirable, it meant less to me compared with the simple love of a father, but I knew better, as my mother later needlessly took pains to remind me. My father's art, including at least to some degree how others thought of it, mattered a lot to him. One suspects the same is true for many artists.

German philosopher Friedrich Nietzsche articulated the philosophical foundation in death for giving art, and the aesthetic value on which art depends, such a central role. As law professor Brian Leiter writes in his book *Nietzsche on Morality* and a chapter *The Truth Is Terrible* in another book of similar title, if, as so many believe, life is only meaningless suffering followed by annihilating death, one's only hope is to find aesthetic value in one's meager existence. Art can, Nietzsche held, anesthetize the pain of life's meaninglessness, seducing one back to life in a sort of sexualized aesthetic, one that at its best, when liberated from morality, becomes a *spectacle of genius*. Nietzsche took as examples of such genius Goethe in literature, Beethoven in music, and Napoleon in politics. One who like Nietzsche imagines living only organically among other animal material, denying the immense order on which aesthetic itself builds, which is what more-conventional thinkers would call morality, must then draw seduction from the senses. Art can certainly seduce, just as can music, literature, sex, drugs, power, money, and many other things. Nietzsche chose the seduction, dying a syphilitic mad man, writing at the end of his life to his concerned friends that he had created the world.

Pop artist Andy Warhol made his own interesting artistic contribution to public thought about death, indeed to the public policy of capital punishment, with his series of large prints and smaller prints and paintings of the electric chair. The public did not know Warhol for his political views or as a social critic. His pop art of soup cans and other consumer products, and celebrity portraits, seemed about as apolitical as one could possibly make art. Yet then, just after a state governor commuted all death sentences in the state, Warhol staged his electric-chair exhibition. Warhol denied, implausibly to art and social critics, that he was making any political or other statement at all in doing so. He was, he maintained, just reproducing images. His exhibition, though, generated the discussion that social critics plausibly assumed Warhol in fact intended. Art, as law professor Bennett Capers observed in a law review article on Warhol's electric-chairs exhibition, has a powerfully dialogic capability, concretizing images that words can only imagine. Indeed, Warhol appears to have based the series on the Sing Sing Prison electric chair in which New York executed Julius and Ethel Rosenberg, with thousands protesting outside, for conspiring to commit espionage during the height of the 1950s red scares. Staring at the colorful printed empty electric chairs nearly forces the viewer into the chair.

The pursuit of meaning in art may be especially acute for the serial killer, as Ricarda Vidal suggests in his chapter *The Power of Negative Creation—Why Art by Serial Killers Sells*, in the book *The Power of Death*. Serial killers Charles Manson, John Wayne Gacy, Henry Lee Lucas, and Richard Ramirez, all turned to creating prison art while serving their multiple life sentences. Bearing the physical burden of legal guilt, if not guilt's mental and emotional burdens, they turned to painting clowns, as in Gacy's case, or creating other works, for relief and distraction if not atonement. Or maybe they create art for the money or notoriety. Their works sell for anything from a few hundred to many thousands of dollars. Shows featuring the works of these and other serial killers make the point of identifying for patrons the artists' crimes including the number of murders. One finds it hard to say which is the stranger phenomenon, the killer creating or the patron buying the creation. Vidal cites others suggesting that the West's suppression of death from public view and consideration simply comes roaring back in violent literature, art, and film. The more we shut it out, the more it attracts us.

John Horne, in the chapter *Screening the Dying Individual: Film, Mortality and the Ethics of Spectatorship*, from the book *The Power of Death*, seconds Vidal's premise that we simply can't keep ourselves from examining death, in Horne's subject, by making film of it. Sex, particularly in the Victorian age we assume, was once taboo and thus a voyeur's tempting subject. With sex about as out in the open in modern society as one can make it, death may be the new taboo. And so out in the open come the art, literature, and films of death, in a voyeur's fashion, as Horne observes, like a new pornography. Horne's questions about the ethics of viewing another's death ring especially keen in the age of social media, when murderers inexplicably post their hideous work for all to see on Facebook, which then almost equally as hideously garners millions of views. Of course, depictions of death need not be violent, voyeuristic, or pornographic but can instead be extraordinarily gentle and sensitive. They can also be authentic and truthful, perhaps even hopeful and inspirational.

Film has indeed contributed its own substantial reflections on dying and death, from the redemptive, as in depictions of Dickens' *A Christmas Carol*, to the ribald, as in Monty Python's *The Life of Brian*. In the latter film, Brian was the reluctant messiah whose companion dying on the cross next to him sang simply that *Life is quite absurd/ And death's the final word/... When you look at it/ Life's a laugh and death's a joke, it's true....* At the other end of the spectrum from Monty Python's deliberately absurd, Carl Theodor Dreyer was among the first and most-successful filmmakers to explore reasons for living and dying, and depicting a frightful manner of death, in the 1928 silent French film *The Passion of Joan of Arc*. Rated as one of the best films ever, *The Passion* followed transcripts of Joan's heresy trial, where she faced and accepted burning at the stake, the film depicting her soul rising in flames to heaven. Dreyer much later made another cinematographic masterpiece *Ordet (The Word)* dealing with faith, death, and resurrection. Thus, film can run the gamut from serious to non-serious treatment of the subjects of dying and death. Indeed, Hollywood's oeuvre on mortality is so plentiful and broad that one can hardly do more than pick and choose for various meaning, which may be the power of art in film that it serves to open as many doors as it closes.

Hollywood may in earlier years have been reluctant to portray much about causes of death or related extreme suffering, producing more feel-good films such as *Knute Rockne, All American,* with the famous scene of character George Gip, played by Ronald Reagan, urging his Notre Dame team to win one for the dying Gipper, and *The Pride of the Yankees*, around Lou Gehrig's demise. Popular film tended to obscure dying and death in gauzy mystery. Yet Hollywood has more recently made explicit films about causes of death, from executions (for example, *The Crucible, Cat Ballou,* and *Hang 'Em High*) to assassinations (*Apocalypse Now, The Jackal,* and *Inglorious Basterds*), euthanasia (*The Bramble Bush* and *You Don't Know Jack*), murder (*Witness, Throw Momma from the Train,* and *Oldboy*), suicide (*Bad Dreams, Reuben, Reuben,* and *Checking Out*), AIDS (*Philadelphia*), killer sharks (*Jaws* and *Great White*), zombies (*World War Z*), aliens (*Alien*), terrorists (*Die Hard*), genocides (*Genocide* and *Hotel Rwanda*), and, yes, natural causes. Films have addressed not only the causes of death but the process of dying (*As I Lay Dying, Dying Young,* and *Dying of the Light*), process of grieving (*Manchester by the Sea*), experience of the afterlife (*What Dreams May Come*), and communication with the dead (*Always* and *Ghost*). Films have also represented widows (*Sleepless in Seattle* and *Beyond Belief*), orphans (*The Golden Compass* and *Free Willy*), murderers (*In the Heat of the Night* and *The Art of Dying*) including mass murderers (*Manson* and *Gacy*), and the innocent but wrongfully accused (*12 Angry Men*) and wrongfully convicted (*The Green Mile*).

Film plainly makes an exquisite and powerful art within which to explore the subjects of living, dying, and death, from abundant perspectives. Ingmar Bergman confirmed his renowned reputation as a film director with 1957's *The Seventh Seal* in which actor Max Von Sydow, playing a medieval knight facing the plague, conducts a film-long game of chess with personified death. The film's title refers to the passage in the Bible's book Revelation in which God remained silent for a half hour after the Lamb had opened the seventh and last seal. The film draws powerfully on well-known traditional, historical, and theological symbols and concepts. In stark contrast, the much-more-recent dystopian science-fiction film *Blade Runner* follows a group of robots trying to extend their artificial expiration date, while chased by a human detective who must confront his own impending natural death. Who should decide, the film invites the audience to ask, the lifespans of human-like androids and human clones? Films can thus confront questions of life's impermanence, feared futility, and ultimate meaning, through either familiar or unfamiliar forms. Film can be especially effective when mixing the familiar with the folkloric, as in the film series depicting J. R. R. Tolkien's *Lord of the Rings* trilogy, which have mortals interacting with immortals, while attempting to forestall, hasten, or shape apocalyptic ends.

Art may thus have greater ability than science and medicine to explore in open, informing, and inspiring ways the meaning and practice of life, dying, and death. Science and medicine involve method, convention, and general acceptance, and are technological pursuits. By contrast, art questions method, challenges convention, and lies just outside of general acceptance, as more than a technological pursuit. Art does not face the bounds of science and medicine. Art can address the whole of our condition, including our imagination, yearning, and spirit, rather than just our material condition. Art can pursue and represent the transcendent. It can speak to the historical and social, the emotional and experiential, and the qualitative over the quantitative. Art does not require proof and does not ground itself in the empirical and testable but instead takes the world as it comes, full of possibility, with an eye to the creative and anomalous. Art imagines the world as it could be, as hints of history have suggested its possibility. Art imagines us within reach of the other side of death.

~

She slumped deep in her rolling office chair, plainly exhausted simply by the effort of being at work, not that she was doing anything more to exhaust herself than sitting and chatting. She hadn't been to work much for the past month or two, barely able to make it in between nauseating and exhausting chemotherapy sessions. Her doctors had more-or-less told her that the chemotherapy was not a cure for her last-stage cancer, instead just to slow her inevitable demise. She had suspected so, well before the doctors had told her. Yet she wanted to be at work where she could still somehow feel a part of life's great arc, which may just be sharing little arcs with others. Late in life, she had cared for people at work in ways that she could no longer care for family, all grown or gone. In her swift demise, her work colleagues had cared for her like family, driving her to chemotherapy sessions, sitting with her through those sessions, and even caring for her overnight at home. In one of those last home visits, she shared with her closest work colleague that she did not fear death but was instead more curious, long comforted as she had been with her destiny's assurance. And then, she was gone, her work colleagues sharing memorial stories of her loving embrace of each of them as their own lives tracked their own terminal arcs toward disparate destinies that each would choose.

5

Death and Music

We played the pipe for you, and you did not dance; we sang a dirge, and you did not mourn.

Matthew 11:17.

Music has challenged, informed, and consoled the living about dying, death, and the dead, likely for as long as humankind has partaken of it. The requiem, as one remotely familiar example, has existed for hundreds of years as a musical form to help the living grieve and memorialize the passage of the dead. Catholic masses for the dead have been held for a millennium, their texts chanted or sung in plain requiem. Hundreds of years ago, the Catholic Church standardized liturgical texts into requiem masses, complex and multi-part in their distinct musical genre, and traditionally in Latin. With their increasing sophistication, requiems arose specifically for concert-hall performance. Requiems typically memorialize the death of a prominent individual, while serving also to reconcile survivors and unify families, communities, regions, and nations. Yet requiems have also commemorated the deaths of many at once, in war or from another catastrophe. Requiems are traditionally religious, specifically Christian in hope and symbol, and Catholic in interceding for the dead, but can also be secular, without religious symbol or connotation.

Using music to console takes professional form in the practice of grief therapy. Grief therapist Chava Sekeles writes in her book *Music*

Therapy: Death and Grief of her decades of experience helping patients manage mourning's disabling effects. Her approach involves detailed initial physiological and psychological patient studies followed by the receptive or active music therapy that her studies suggest. Music therapists may treat either the dying patient, easing the anguish of facing looming death, or family members and friends mourning the death of a loved one. She writes, for instance, of gradually drawing out again the tender voice of a child whose mother and baby brother a terrorist attack had killed, and who thus suffered severe post-traumatic stress disorder including mutism. She writes, too, of treating cancer patients who wished in their slow death to absorb as much beauty and serenity as life offered. Sometimes the mourners listen to recorded music, sometimes to music that the therapist herself plays in clinical improvisation. Other times, the mourners compose or play music, even inartfully as laymen. Always, the effort is to help the mourner feel and express feeling against death's cold grip. Sometimes the mourner chooses the music on the therapist's recommendation.

More often the therapist chooses. According to Sekeles, music therapist's choices for treating death's mourners are seldom requiems, which may serve better for public, formal memorials than for private reflection and treatment. The therapist's selections are more often art music, compositions that express various stages of grief. The compositions may reflect denial as in the fourth of Mahler's *Songs on the Death of Children*, anger as in Leonard Bernstein's *Halil*, or dark and depressive solemnity as in Anton Bruckner's *Seventh Symphony*. The selections may also be tender and reconciling, like part three of Gabriel Faure's *Pelleas and Melisande*. The music itself may console out of its alternately raging, solemn, tender, or uplifting forms, while at other times lyrics may better inform the mourner. Alternatively, a single composition like Chopin's *Funeral March*, written by an exquisite composer who suffered exile, tuberculosis, and other hardships before dying at age thirty-eight, can convey the full range of emotions in facing death. Sekeles quotes Oscar Wilde writing in *The Critic as an Artist* that music creates for the mourner "a past of which one has been ignorant and [yet that] fills one with a sense of sorrows that have been hidden from one's tears." Sekeles reports widely different reactions to official mourners' songs, but at its best, when carefully selected, music can elicit consoling memories, filling the mourner with needed emotion while transforming grief's negative energy.

Music, in its exploration of death, reaches well beyond the requiem and grief music. Compositions exploring aspects of death are common among the works of the classical titans. Beethoven wrote from his deathbed his final String Quartet on the *Question of the Existence of the Unknown*, striving to reconcile death with the divine. Bach wrote his greatest *Trauer-Ode Cantata No. 198* for mourners at a queen's funeral and his spiritual masterpiece *St. Matthew Passion* addressing the suffering and death of Christ. After illness exposed his mortality, Schubert composed his bleakly foreboding *Death and the Maiden*. Strauss composed his *Four Last Songs* calmly exploring the cycle of life and accepting his impending death, only to have the compositions named and performed posthumously. Gustav Mahler wrote his *Kindertotenlieder* on the death of poet Friedrich Ruckert's two children, before Mahler's own young daughter died, after which, he said, he could not have composed the songs. Austrian composer Alban Berg wrote the opera *Wozzeck* based on a similarly named play that Georg Buchner left unfinished at his death, addressing through a story of murder and suicide the death and despair that the first World War left. For a modern example depicting death as grindingly material, Birtwistle composed *Triumph of Time* to represent the sixteenth-century work of the same name by Flemish artist Pieter Bruegel the Elder. Avant-garde composer Georg Crumb added *Black Angels*, opposing symbolic movements of the devil and divine around death, written for electric string quartet with register extremes, bowing played above the fingered fretboard, and thimbles tapping the strings.

Songs addressing death, though, are not merely relics of the past or properties solely of the classical. In popular music's vast repository and ready accessibility, one finds musical expression for all manner of attitudes toward death. Professor Christopher Partridge, in his book *Music and Mortality*, examines how popular music today alternately confronts and obscures death, while also transgressing death's cultural conventions, exploring its uncanniness, giving voice to its vortex, and inviting its transcendence. Popular music, in other words, takes as many approaches to death as the market will bear. For his part, for example, Partridge finds unbearable the thought of eternal life and so prefers to see himself dissolving into nothing, as the Incredible String Band evoked in 1967's *My Name Is Death* with the lines *My name is Death, cannot you see? / All life must turn to me.* While despising eternal life, Partridge at the same time believes culture to be the product of the denial and repression of the better fact of death, citing the title of a Wooden Shjips song *Death's Not Your Friend.* Partridge thus favors George Harrison's *All Things Must Pass* album for the poignancy of the line *there'll come a time when all of us must leave here,* in its song *Art of Dying,* but also likes the band It's Immaterial's album *Life's Hard Then You Die.* You can find and listen to what you want.

Whatever your confirmed or developing view of death, music's magical capacity to transport, to alternately project one forward while recalling one's past within the emotion of the present, make it a profound medium to help us countenance death. Partridge insightfully discerns that music creates *affective space*, more than just entertaining, instead helping us construct our identities in a sort of *prosthetic technology.* Notice music's power in these concepts. Partridge lauds that most of us today, and especially the young, accept popular music as purveyor of attitudes and guide to knowledge. Others are more cautious about the benefits of such unfiltered influences, rooted as popular music is in the transitional culture of youth. Partridge helpfully suggests that popular music can court Gothic and other deliberately dark forms in part because Western youths hold death somewhat at arm's length, in contrast to other societies beset by infant mortality, malaria, bad water, infectious diseases, and civil wars, and where the elderly die at home. In openly exploring death, though, popular music may not only be helping us stomach the thought of dying but also to explore related possibilities, Partridge discerns and welcomes, citing reincarnation referenced in Harrison's *All Things Must Pass.*

Popular music in its different genres and songs of course reflects the gamut of beliefs about death, beginning with Partridge's belief in inevitable personal extinction. He cites appreciatively Scottish musician Malcolm Middleton's *We're All Going to Die*, the lyrics of which begin with *what if there's nothing* and then go into a chant of *you're gonna die* ending, finally, with *alone* and then, for emphasis, *all alone*. Everything decays, and thus life's efforts are futile, expressed beautifully, Partridge discerns, in Brian Eno's *Golden Hours*, in that *my brains have turned to sand* as *I've seen the evening slide away / Watching the signs / Taking over from the fading day*. We are biological organisms, the view holds, experience and meaning dissolved forever with the organism. Thus, all striving in life is absurd, banal, and distracting, especially striving to overcome death, because we *came from nothing* and *will all return to nothing*, Partridge concludes confidently, citing the Russian-American novelist Vladimir Nabokov. But, Partridge attempts to cheer us, eternity itself would be meaningless, indeed hellish, as the Talking Heads' song *Heaven* communicates in its lyrics *the band in Heaven plays my favorite song / They play it once again, they play it all night long*, and *when this kiss is over it will start again / It will not be any different, it will be exactly the same*, hence, *Heaven is a place where nothing ever happens*. The value of the thought is, this argument shows, all in how once conceives it.

Partridge's citation of Nabokov to sustain an existentialist's argument is curious because the great Russian-American novelist knew the transcendent. In his story *Beneficence*, Nabokov wrote of the narrator realizing that the world is not *a predaceous sequence of chance events* but instead *shimmering bliss, beneficent trepidation, a gift bestowed on us and unappreciated*. When Nabokov's father died, he wrote his mother that they were *certain* to see his father again *coming towards us in our shared bright eternity*, as Larry Woiwode quotes in *The Stories of Vladimir Nabokov*. *You must live in expectation of that tender hour, my love*, Nabokov continued to write his mother, *and never give in to the temptation of despair* for *everything will return*. Even the reputed existentialist yearns toward eternity.

Partridge contrasts his existentialist belief and the songs that support it, with what he characterizes as the obscuring of death's decay, through cultural denial and psychological protection, reflected in Johnny Cash's *Hymns from the Heart* offered in witness to the life of Christ. Still, songs of hope, whether describing the authentic or imagined, in Partridge's view present opportunities for making meaning of grief. He cites as good examples Michael Gira's *Rose of Los Angeles* articulating the singer's grief over loss of his mother and Cloud Cult Craig Minowa's album *They Live on the Sun* addressing the singer's grief over the sudden death of his son. Minowa even wove audio recordings of his deceased son's voice into his songs *I'm Not Gone* and *Took You for Granted*, the power of which one can sense even before listening to the music. And metaphor, even if inauthentic, can still be powerful, Partridge discerns, as in Rod Stewart's projecting his lover, in the song *You're in My Heart (The Final Acclaim)*, to be timeless and ageless. Indeed, the popular myth of Elvis living extends the metaphor of agelessness beyond the song's subject to the singer. Witness the canonization of seminal artists in other genres, depending on your judgment, like Buddy Holly, Jimi Hendrix, Michael Jackson, and Kurt Cobain, not to mention a certain performer-musician-songwriter who for a time preferred identification by an unpronounceable symbol.

Music need not convey the singer's commitments or inform directly those of the listener, to have a restorative power. Partridge cites as good example Lou Reed's *Magic and Loss* album, as a challenging but helpfully meditative reflection, following the deaths of Reed's songwriter and artist friends. References to small miracles of healing manage to leaven the album's disconcerting depiction of arduous cancer treatment successful only in stealing the sufferer's remaining life. Reed sings in *Power and Glory* that he *saw a great man turn into a little child / The cancer reduced him to dust*. Reed measures the awful impact of the loss in the song *What's Good*, intoning that *now life is like death without living / That's what life's like without you.* The song *Cremation* then deals with the frightening thought that the body is only tiny bits of carbon, *they burnt you up / Collect you in a cup*, relieved only in part in the song *Sword of Damocles* with the possibility *maybe there's something over there / Some other world that we don't know about.* Yet then, other artists like Buck Dharma of Blue Oyster Cult, in *(Don't Fear) The Reaper* expand on the possibility that death is merely a door to a better life. Artists also haven't hesitated to conjure words against death, even in titles like the band Years' *Hey Cancer... F--- You!*

Music's not-so-subtle capacity for transgressing social norms and cultural conventions, reflected in the prior song title's profanity, is another reason that it can serve as a powerful accompaniment for reflections on dying and death. Partridge gives as primary examples the band Smog's *Dress Sexy at My Funeral* and Alice Cooper's *I Love the Dead*, the latter forcing the listener into proximity with the thought of the recently dead's still-warm but necrosing flesh. At concerts, Cooper would stage the impaling of babies, Ozzy Osbourne would bite off a bat's head, and Mayhem would impale sheep's heads on stakes. What one artist does, another must outdo. The band Mortician's song *Intro / Defiler of the Dead* embraces full-on necrophilia, while the band Cannibal Corpse in songs like *A Skull Full of Maggots* revels in explicit imagery of decaying flesh.

Yet popular music's transgression goes well beyond ignoring taboos having to do with treatment of the dead, to the point of profaning sacral approaches to dying and death. Perhaps no band has done so more pointedly than Christian Death, with albums like *Sex and Drugs and Jesus Christ*, *Sexy Death God*, *Pornographic Messiah*, and *Born Again Anti Christian*. The band's founding member Roz Williams eventually succumbed in unfortunate suicide to the bloody red death about which he so transgressively and with such fascination sang. Christian Death is in no sense unique, though, in music annals. The Japanese doom metal band Church of Misery, in their song *Doctor Death* on their album *And Then There Were None*, solicited killer drugs from England's notorious serial-killer physician Harold Shipman, interspersing the song with clips of news broadcasts about Shipman's criminal conviction for fifteen of his estimated two-hundred-fifty murders.

While we define transgressions as things that one ought to resist and condemn, questioning the value of the above examples, music still seems at its best capable of opening conventions, even sacred conventions, to fresh examination, even fresh life. One has at times to find one's self in the dark to see the light. Partridge gives one a framework within which to think about popular music's transgression of the sacred through images of death. Most children in the West lead highly structured lives, as do adults. Youth maturing into adulthood, though, go through a chaotic, unstructured transition. Transitions from stage to stage, whether youth to adulthood, school to job, unmarried to married, childless to with-children, or, for that matter, life to death, require, or if you prefer *permit*, subcultures. When in transition, one stands against the culture one leaves and yet apart from the culture that one prepares to join. To provide a sort of substitute authenticity during a transition that has no order or norm, transitional subcultures identify themselves using transgression and extremes. Youths adopt transgressive popular music for identity, status, and meaning during a period that supplies none of those needs. That the transgressive extremes of popular music may be mostly inauthentic, merely songs and album-cover art, not true homicide and necrophilia, doesn't diminish their usefulness, instead making them appropriate to serve in transition. Indeed, their inauthenticity may soon endorse for the maturing youth the *authenticity* of the meanings, forms, and truths that they challenge. Let's hope so, or God help America.

Some hold that transgressive listeners are earning more subcultural capital listening to popular Gothic music about the uncanny and undead. Partridge identifies the genre-defining classic as the song *Black Sabbath* by the band of the same, distinctly transgressive name, like that also of Black Widow. The affective space that cover art, sounds, and words create, referencing an old mill, church graveyard, and funeral, with torrents of rain and peels of thunder, fill with half-living, haunted and spectral images. Appreciate that these dark but still-numinous images are not modern, secular, or existential but instead ancient, romantic, and spiritual. That these Gothic forms and references are primarily satanic does not reject but instead impliedly endorses that one could discover and embrace the competing salvific entity. Gothic forms are a reaction against what Partridge properly labels *brutal modernity*, perhaps much more so than profane claims against the sacred. Gothic once threatened the sacred but instead now saves the sacred from the searing modern secular mind. Indeed, Partridge describes how the band Depeche Mode, singer Johnny Cash, and singer Marilyn Manson each gave the same song *Personal Jesus* such different meaning, the first secular, the second Christian, and the last profane, simply in the arrangement, accompaniment, and staging.

Music so effectively creates these affective spaces that the artist can imbue and listener discern starkly different understandings of living, dying, and death, even from the same song. Popular music at its best creates these spaces, bringing dying to the fore in an otherwise unhealthily antiseptic culture, so that we can deal with our mortality out in the light where these highest-stakes investigations belong. Not all artists do so in a socially and culturally transgressive manner. For example, Bono, lead singer of the band U2, accepts the challenge for the open examination of the question of death and possibility that it entails, without veering into what adherents to the traditional might see as sacrilegious. Pastor theologian Timothy Keller, leading the six-thousand-member Redeemer Church in Manhattan and author of *The Reason for God*, quotes Bono as examining the secular response to accounts of Jesus's resurrection and the possibility of our own resurrection when we embrace him. Bono notes that one cannot simply accept Jesus as a deluded but nonetheless wise prophet. Jesus instead forces one to decide: if a lunatic, then reject him, but if the incarnate and resurrected God as he claimed, then center your life around him. Bono, for a notably popular and influential musician, leaves open that possibility of confronting mortality in trust of the man-God.

Other composers and musicians have pursued with lifelong passion that possibility of dealing with death through the one who died to defeat it. Swiss classical composer Frank Martin, born in 1890 and composing into the 1970s, let a marriage of the musical and spiritual help him deal with the death of his young wife, the carnage of two World Wars, and his own mortality, in the course writing compositions that orchestras continue to play the world over. As musicologist Siglind Bruhn charts in her book *Frank Martin's Musical Reflections on Death*, music opened to Martin truths that he had been unable to put into words or thoughts, and unable to express other than through music. His revelation first occurred when he set to music Christ's passion. Yet Martin would go on to write notable classical compositions addressing death as penalty for fatal pursuits in *The Potion*, as fulfillment of heroic glory in *The Cornet*, as wrathful judge in *Everyman*, as the consequence of war in *In Terra Pax*, as boundary overcome in *Golgotha*, and finally in his own *Requiem*.

In the latter work, written near the end of his life, Martin professed to make peace with death, both its physical travail and the moral anguish one feels over not having made more of life, while still retaining confidence in eternal rest won through earnest prayer for the mercy that rest requires. Throughout, Martin hesitated to overreach his expertise, relying instead on the shelter of commissions within which he could simply do his best without presuming to promote ostensibly great work. Humility before death and, moreover, before the Lord who would save him from it, was his life's work. Martin wrote his last composition, a cantata with the translated title *And Life Won the Day*, interrupted by several illnesses as he rushed to finish what he in the end knew would be his final work. The composition at first implies what all must feel in approaching death, an acute sense of estrangement from humanity's warmth, before rising gently to reflect a glorious peace found in the fullness of life precisely as death relieved by grace informs it.

~

The musician, an ordinary bass-guitar player, as most bass-guitar players are ordinary or, if better than ordinary, still prefer to be thought so, hadn't expected the unusual gig. The enormously successful and beloved high-school basketball coach, devoted husband to an equally devoted wife and father of extraordinary but still-maturing young men, had died suddenly, utterly unexpectedly on a daily run, while in the center of community and prime of life. Hundreds of students, teachers, friends, and family packed the summer-weekday funeral service at the coach's contemporary church in a beautifully restored old warehouse, so many as to line the walls standing in the back. The coach's wife had selected two contemporary songs for the service. The church's band leader had put out the call for volunteers to play, but only the band leader on acoustic guitar, bass player, and lead soprano vocalist were available, when the band usually played with several more musicians and vocalists. The spare trio took the stage at their moment in the packed service, the band leader pausing to let everyone gather their thoughts. Then the music began, spare, yes, but somehow otherworldly, transcendent and transporting in the way that only music can be. The heavens opened, and angels sang in welcome of another soul who had glorified the One who would save him.

6

Death and Culture

Remember him—
before the silver cord is severed,
and the golden bowl is broken;
before the pitcher is shattered at the spring,
and the wheel broken at the well,
and the dust returns to the ground it came from,
and the spirit returns to God who gave it.

Ecclesiastes 12:6-7.

    Cultures present the richest mix of practices around death and dying. Whatever you can imagine, one culture or another has probably adopted, passed down through the generations, and repeatedly done. Take for example the disposition of the body. Burial may seem a dominant Western practice, until one considers the high frequency of cremations, with the cremated remains offered to the family in an urn for even more-widespread variation in practices. Cremations account for one third of funerals in the United States, with wide variation in cremation rates from state to state, Nevada leading at two thirds and Mississippi trailing at under ten percent. The variation in cremation rates is even greater internationally, with some countries like Nepal and Japan at over ninety-five percent and other countries like Ireland and Poland under ten percent. Cost and availability of burial versus cremation or other rites affect the dying and their family members' choices, as do spiritual beliefs and, as this chapter addresses, culture in its rituals, superstitions, taboos, practices, and traditions. Culture has no obligation to explain its practices, yet the choice of burial versus cremation finds other rationales beyond cost and availability, in things such as preserving the body as a spiritual vehicle or, conversely, ensuring that the body's decomposition does not interfere with the health of the surviving soul.

Other cultures offer alternative funeral rites. Exposure of the body on open high ground in sky burial allows scavenger birds to carry bits of the body aloft, nearer heaven, while saving precious fuel wasted in pyre or arduous digging for burial. In contrast, embalming using chemicals to slow decay of the flesh or mummification to dry the body for preservation preserves the body for veneration or spiritual abode. Burials at sea serve fishing cultures or maritime traditions, while launch of the remains in space orbit, of which dozens have partaken, celebrates that extraordinary new technological capability. Commitment of the body to medicine for organ transplant or other organic harvesting serves the living, while commitment of the body to science serves the future. Some remote cultures even reportedly hang the bodies in the woods. Various cultures and subcultures around the globe vary widely in their practices for disposing, thoughtfully and swiftly, of the deteriorating body, which because of that deterioration is a compelling necessity.

Don't underestimate the power of culture in influencing the disposition of human remains. Animal-rights advocate Carmen Cusack advocates in her article *Death Revolution* that modern societies should adopt the practice, thankfully witnessed only rarely among cultures worldwide, of eating the dead. Better for the animals whose meat the human remains would replace, Cusack argues, and better for the environment than cremation or burial. The sacred, ritual, moral, and spiritual views that would cause us to resist such consumption are only antiquated views, Cusack holds, although she does resist killing the living for consumption, as she reports that certain healers in Tanzania evidently do.

Setting aside the bizarre, the attention that funeral rites give to the body's proper disposition fulfills at least two functions for the survivors who care for the dead, family researcher Martin Richards and reproductive-sciences professor Martin Johnson discern in their chapter *Death Writes* in the book *Death Rites and Rights*. On one hand, families wish to give their dead relatives the proverbial *good sendoff* while simultaneously ensuring that the dead *rest in peace*, a function focusing on the interest of the dead. On the other hand, families use last rites for their own immediate interest in disposing of the body while remembering, memorializing, and celebrating the life of the dead. Thus, whatever funeral practices one finds within a certain culture, one may see interwoven these two functions of theoretical respect for the dead and practical treatment of the body, in the context of community remembrance. Richards and Johnson identify as evidence of these goals that families will often go to great lengths to recover bodies, body parts, or even small bits of body tissue to inter, while also objecting vigorously to any action, such as autopsy or organ harvest, that deprives the family of a full interment. Families or officials may alternatively *divide* the body to inter in not one but two locations of significance, as was the case for poet Thomas Hardy whose heart lies interred at a Dorset church but with the cremated rest of his remains interred in the Poet's Corner of Westminster Abbey.

Other cultural practices can be significant, no matter the body's ultimate disposition. Whether buried or cremated, the body may first receive ritual bathing, oiling, and dressing or, conversely, no touch at all while the soul or spirit transitions. Cultures may also promote ancestor worship including offerings of food, clothing, money, and prayer, especially where ancestors are thought to bless or curse the living. Tending the grave or ground of the dead may be a part of that ritual, which may also include an annual celebration of the Day of the Dead. Ritual may even dictate how and to whom clinicians announce the death, and with what detail as to its cause. Culture will also affect the mourners' response, whether in wailing announcing the degree to which the survivors loved the departed one or in nearly complete restraint out of respect for the moment's profundity and in show of courage. Culture may further dictate quite different responses for different sexes or classes of mourners.

Culture can also affect the course of dying and cause of death, most starkly in those cultures that have encouraged or tolerated human sacrifice. Animal sacrifice remains a significant practice in certain cultures such as those influenced by Islam when celebrating a two-day sacrifice feast requiring the slaughter of as many as 100 million animals. Human sacrifice, relatively common among certain ancient cultures including the pre-Columbian Aztec, Inca, and Mayans, the Middle Eastern Canaanites, and the Near East Carthaginians and Phoenicians, criminal laws generally forbid today, although children and others still die at the hands of witch doctors, healers, and others, even their parents. Parental infanticide, while officially discouraged even in countries adhering to one-child policies, likely continues to contribute to infant deaths, especially among females, adding to a sex imbalance in those populations. Infant deaths declined significantly in the United States in the years following abortion's legalization, some assert due to a decrease in parental infanticide.

Somewhere in this rich or, in the latter cases of human sacrifice and infanticide, sordid mix of cultural practices, Americans have lost too much of their ability to deal with death through ritual. Cultural anthropologist Donald Joralemon writes in his book *Mortal Dilemmas* that medical advances have flipped the ritualized transition period from life to death. A person used to die, followed by ritual mourning in forms that the culture strongly supported. Biological death preceded social death, as a natural order would seem most appropriate. Now, however, medicine keeps terminally ill patients alive but entirely withdrawn from their social networks. Social death now occurs before, rather than after, biological death. Thus, mourning must now precede death, leaving death itself, what was once the sudden and seminal event, an anticlimax. Culture has not yet helped us perfect substitute pre-death rituals for the medically absent, to take the place of the funerals and wakes that helped us cope in the past. So, we have no way either to mourn the long, slow, but certain decline toward death or the death itself that quietly and anticlimactically follows. Culture has lost its ability to help us cope with medically managed decline, unless one has a personal chronicler like author Mitch Albom serving professor Morrie Schwartz, documented in the book *Tuesdays with Morrie*.

You may even have experienced one of these new odd moments that cultural anthropologist Joralemon calls *gradual-onset pre-mortem liminality*. Liminality involves a transitional stage with one foot in each camp across a divide, in this instance the divide between life and death. You may have, in diagnosis of a life-threatening condition, experienced a small part, a glimmer perhaps, of your social death preceding biological death. People begin speaking of you as if you are not there. The doctor bearing the bad news speaks of average survival duration and other figures, helpful maybe but still reducing the patient to number sets. Family members speak to one another, yes, of care and support needs for the dying one who listens in but then, *no!* of plans after the dying one passes. Medically managed dying can make the patient invisible, isolated, and lonely, particularly when culture has not yet developed helpful rituals, practices, and routines to support the terminal but not-yet-dead patient. Some have applied the concept of social death much more broadly, for instance to those whose criminal conviction requires them to register as a sex offender, as law professor Elizabeth Berenguer argues in her article *The Invisible Man*, isolating them to the point of social invisibility. But the isolation of social death is especially acute when a terminal illness makes family, friends, and professionals treat one as if already dead.

Other cultural and demographic trends impact mourning, a practice from which we once learned and drew so much but for which we may now find less time. Joralemon notes the impact of two-earner households, where neither member has the time to nurture the rituals of passing, for personal and household benefit, not to mention the departed one's memory and legacy. Bury mom on Saturday, back to work Monday. Workplaces pretend competence in grief care. We even hold workplace memorials and funeral services, three of them in my current workplace, with flowers, printed remembrance, music, exhortation, eulogy, guests, food, and all. The only thing missing each time was the body, not that workplace memorials provide an equivalent experience to a home or church service, leaving, as the workplace inevitably does, the implication that the moment the service concludes, one must get back to work. The mourners, like the recently departed, also see their grief medicalized, with professional counselors and even medication replacing social support and ritual. Joralemon argues that in this changing context, we need new cultural scripts, perhaps as the workplace memorial attempts to serve.

One way that a material culture like ours deals with death is through the material. Professor of material culture Daniel Miller and anthropologist Fiona Parrott, in their chapter *Death, Ritual, and Material Culture* in the book *Death Rites and Rights*, note how survivors use different objects in different ways to fulfill their memorial needs. A departed loved one's necklace, worn close to the survivor's heart, may serve a consoling remembrance function. A piece of the departed one's clothing may envelop the wearer with the loved one's look, feel, and even smell. Photographs, of course, carry the dead into the survivor's new lives, homes, and relationships. Old music the dead had shared, and new music making new references to the old relationship, revivify the departed to the survivor. Special recipes that the dead had shared, even homemade wines, offer their own communion. We use these objects and goods in informal but tangible ritual, every bit as meaningful as the words and song of a funeral service, reminding one another of the departed one's presence, commitments, character, and value. An estate sale of the departed one's humble treasures becomes a day-long celebration of profound humanity discovered again in the mundane. We preserve and parcel out to family members and friends the sentimental objects, reconstituting the dead not as a generic ancestor but unique and personal material presence.

Cemeteries, like the use of personal physical objects, also reflect how culture treats death. The cemetery adjacent to which my wife and I have lived for most of thirty years, onto which our back windows and deck look, the city laid out 150 years earlier as a place for families to gather at the gravesites for picnics after church on Sunday. The oldest gravesites show evidence of that intent, with marble benches and borders to ensure that the living families had their space and comfort around the headstones. One can imagine the buggies parked nearby, with the tethered or hobbled horses grazing on the beautiful hillsides. The couple-hundred-acre cemetery occupies some of the most gorgeous rolling dunes in the state, right in the dense city's heart. Today, those dunes would be covered in mini-mansions if they were available for development. Back then, the citizens expected the dunes to be covered in their treasured dead, for their frequent convenient visit. Skateboarders, bicyclists, runners, and dog walkers use the cemetery today. I sometimes wonder what they think of exercising and recreating in the presence of so many dead, but my wife and I have lived there so long that doing so just seems natural. Only new visitors to our home give a strange look at the gorgeous cemetery, and shiver.

Historian Philippe Aries in his book *The Hour of Our Death* traces how Western culture has changed over time in its disposal of human remains. At times, disposal was in or about the home, perhaps under the dirt floor or discretely tucked away, safe from scavenging animals. At other times, burials in fields, not grand but rather low and indiscrete places, were haphazard, with little concern shown for the depth and permanency of the disposal. Gradually, hygiene and propriety demanded, and prosperity permitted, greater ceremony and structure in outdoor disposal of remains. Those who could afford it arranged for burial in elaborate underground vaults, while others found and used natural tombs. A period passed when those who had the influence and means arranged not for outdoor burial in cemeteries but for interment in funerary chapels or tombs within churches. Ornate mosaics carpeted the marble floors of some churches, memorializing the prominent departed parishioners whose remains lay beneath, while painted angels adorned the ceiling overhead. Humility eventually demanded interment below plain flush slabs, first indoors and gradually outdoors again, in the churchyard with the poor. The settlement of America embraced that practice of outdoor burial either in a cemetery on the homestead or, if reasonably convenient, then in the churchyard. Graves of the poor bore no adornment, while those who died with means adorned graves with usually modest, although sometimes ornate, slabs, headstones, or steles.

While one hears that popular culture, so enamored of youth and health, conceals dying in nursing homes and death in antiseptic hospitals, we have good indications of living instead in a culture of death. Television features the fictional *CSI: Crime Scene Investigation*, with dead bodies, body parts, and related forensics front and center. With fictionalized depictions of death and the dead not enough to fulfill our appetites, television features a decade-long series *Autopsy* exploring famous and infamous deaths, culminating in a step-by-step actual autopsy as the medical-examiner host reminisces on difficult past cases. *Actual Autopsy* on-demand video then garners over one-hundred-million views. The genre then moves swiftly on to *celebrity* autopsies, charting the last hours of Michael Jackson, Whitney Houston, and other entertainers who suffered suspicious, sudden, and unfortunate, rather than plainly natural, demise. A reality television series *Family Plots*, shot in a funeral home, makes the cadaver the star. And if video is not enough, then come see the traveling exhibit of real corpses in *Body Worlds*. The real-or-fake remains that were once discrete carnival side shows are now readily available for us to consume without either sacredness or shame. Scholar Jacque Lynn Foltyn, in her chapter *Dead Sexy: Why Death Is the New Sex* in the book *Making Sense of Death, Dying and Bereavement*, writes that we live in *the corpse's cultural moment*. Culture divorces emotion and sensibility from the dead body's relentless exploitation, in pornographic embrace. Secular, material culture has utterly commoditized the dead body, around which the material unliving now hover, forgetting that the dead should remind them of their own impending death.

The internet facilitates the culture's exposure, exploration, and desacralizing of death. The anthology *Making Sense of Death, Dying and Bereavement* collects evidence of what the internet offers, starting with personal web memorials, sometimes the dead person's web page resurrected as memorial and other times special pages created by family, funeral home, or friends. Some of these pages encourage public posts, supporting strings commenting on the departed one's life and mourning the death. Websites support virtual memorial gardens, little plaque images bearing names, birth dates, and dates of death, in loving memory. Who knows but that these virtual images might outlast the inscribed gravestones? Longer posts recount the dearly departed one's greatest achievements, greater wishes, and last days, or details of the memorial service, including who spoke and who didn't speak. Special websites gather stories of cancer battles or other paths to demise. One government-supported effort even published photographs of unidentified dead persons for family to peruse and identify, following a devastating tsunami.

The internet of course offers abundant resources and contacts for support around dying, death, and bereavement, including helplines, discussion forums, message boards, online counseling, and compassion training, and referrals to caregivers and foundations. Not all internet depictions are healthy. Teens and young adults visit internet chat rooms to learn preferable methods for suicide. Suspicions arise that cyber-suicides, internet-promoted and memorialized, even imitate art, for example around the suicide that Goethe's 1774 novel *The Sorrows of Young Werther* depicted, purporting to lend some meaning, or at least some notoriety, to an otherwise senseless death.

What internet service providers may or must do with a deceased person's social-media accounts is also a significant cultural issue, both around privacy interests and property interests, the latter when an account had many followers from whom the decedent formerly drew commercial or other value. The law-review article *What Happens to Our Facebook Accounts When We Die?* draws the tension among a dying individual's wishes to control social-media rights beyond death, social-media provider policies attempting to maintain order, and state probate laws trying to ensure efficient administration of property rights after death. The problem, although perhaps only a first-world concern, may be larger than one thinks. The article estimates that 580,000 Facebook users die annually. The trend, although still uncertain and fluid, is toward the probate-appointed executor's traditional control of the decedent's social-media accounts like other estate assets. While we often have little control over the timing and terms of our biological death, by choosing and instructing a responsible executor, one can control to some degree the terms of one's digital death, within a popular culture obsessed with social media.

Indeed, a last will and testament is itself both a legal and cultural convention. Law ordinarily looks to a will for direction as to how to treat the dead person's assets and debts. Law may also give some weight to the decedent's wishes as to who, in the absence, inability, or death of both parents, care for the decedent's minor children. In the absence of a will, law presumes certain preferences, although persons generally find it better to make their own will rather than let the state make decisions for them. Yet wills follow their own cultural conventions. They generally do not, for instance, reflect much of anything other than the law's language and lawyer's voice as to the maker's intentions. A will, as Americans treat it, is solely a legal rather than personal or memorial document. Persons who wish to convey something personal and memorial in their passing will, with or without the help of a lawyer, also make out funeral and memorial plans. Some lawyers help their elderly clients record video messages to loved ones to view after the client's decease, vastly improving communication of last encouragement, over a will's dry legal language.

Public-policy issues relating to death also influence popular culture. For many, abortion weighs on the nation's conscience, fifty-eight million and counting in the United States alone. We may soon ask how history will judge a nation that gave up one-hundred million of its own. Europe brags of nearly extinguishing persons with Downs syndrome, approaching a 100% abortion rate. Is eliminating the less productive, the abnormal, something of which to be proud? Public-policy issues relating to death extend to the end of life, where we meet Dr. Death driving his van filled with euthanasia equipment, out for house calls. Offered as a compassionate response to the terminally and painfully ill, euthanasia may instead wrap its cold hand around the throats of those who don't find their life worth living. In some Western countries, euthanasia is no longer just for the terminally ill but available also to the depressed or even to the unwilling disabled. Doctors practice euthanasia locally on disabled infants in the Netherlands under controversial protocol, where post-birth abortion and euthanasia uncomfortably meet.

Suicide also remains a significant social, cultural, mental-health, and public-policy issue. That suicide rates, currently about thirteen per one hundred thousand, vary widely by age, sex, economic cycles, geographic region, and other demographics confirms that society and culture influence its incidence. American men, for instance, currently commit suicide at over three times the rate of women. Men in their fifties have recently shown a fifty percent rise in suicides to a rate two-and-a-half times the national average, while women in their sixties have shown a sixty percent rise. Adult suicide rates in the most recent decade showed a thirty percent increase. Middle-aged white men are the most likely to take their own lives, although Native Americans of all ages and both sexes slightly outpace the overall white suicide rates. Black, Asian, and Hispanic Americans are less than half as likely to commit suicide. About forty-five-thousand Americans die to suicide every year, more than die in motor-vehicle accidents annually and approaching the total number of Americans dying in the Vietnam War. Suicide is the tenth leading cause of U.S. deaths, costing $51 billion annually, at the rate of one-hundred-twenty-one suicides per day. For every suicide, twenty-five more survivors have attempted suicide, the total loss, pain, and disruption of lives incalculable.

Nearly half of U.S. suicides involve the use of a firearm. My law practice once involved me in a dispute over the death of a business man who shot himself with a shotgun. The clothes that he had worn, bloodied and shot-ridden, weirdly ended up at the center of the dispute. Death, especially sudden and violent death, can dramatically and unpredictably change the relationships of survivors, and often for the worse rather than the better. Suffocation and poisoning are the next most-common suicide methods. Despite the large number and high rate of U.S. suicides, the country ranks only around fiftieth, near the bottom of the top third, on suicide rates among one-hundred-eighty countries keeping statistics. Sri Lankans commit suicide at nearly three times the U.S. rate and South Koreans at twice the U.S. rate, while Icelanders at about the same as the U.S. rate, Mexicans at about half the U.S. rate, and Jamaicans, famously happy, at only about one-tenth the U.S. rate. Culture indeed influences death rates.

Culture's influence on attitudes toward death may be at its worst when society's citizens do not share a healthy view of the nature, meaning, and value of life. Psychologist and philosopher Jerry Piven, in his chapter *Ontological Dread* in the book *Unequal Before Death*, discerns ideologies through which culture subtly rationalizes who should live, whom society should value, and who should die. In a material culture, for instance, celebrity and wealth tend to determine one's social value, leading citizens not only to show their perceived inferiors disdain but also to treat life as a slippery commodity to hoard and envy in Darwinian struggle against one another. If life is not being, or an intrinsic process or inherent quality, but instead an entity or essence, then one may contain, transmit, acquire, and consume life, and manipulate and steal life, like other commodities. In Piven's view, commoditizing life as a fantasized tradeable essence promotes violence, fraud, and theft against others whom one believes less deserving of possessing and controlling the quality. Indeed, as a fantasized entity, life when killed, not just like the Aztecs sacrificing neighboring tribesmen but also like the modern narcissist sucking life from anyone in contact, may fructify the life of the executioners in a sort of ritualized scapegoating.

A proper attitude toward death can, on the other hand, help us produce healthier politics and culture. In a view that art historian and lecturer Chris Townsend in his book *Art and Death* draws from philosophers Georges Bataille and Jacques Derrida, among others, proper attitude toward death binds us in broader social and political relationship than traditional notions of equality and fraternity. That deeper cultural fellowship arises out of healthy reflection on death. As we befriend and care for one another, we know how temporary is our time together and that one of us will die before the other. One may even suspect that friendship only bears its full fruit when one dies, leaving the other to bury the dead while carrying on the legacy and memory. Memorials are not, at their best, letting go of fellowship but instead sealing the final pact of fellowship. Strong politics and culture thus arise only out of the intergenerational commitments that death enables, not out of the transactional nature of mere fraternity, which one side is too often ready to sacrifice when the advantage arises.

One's view of the culture, whether healthy or not in its attitudes toward killing, dying, and death, thus likely depends on one's deeper commitments, understanding, morals, and experience. The signal point about culture today may be that one cannot escape it. As philosopher/theologian Dallas Willard writes in *The Divine Conspiracy*, we no longer have, like Tolstoy, a humble peasantry whose ministrations help us preserve our humanity from the random visions of misguided popularizers. Television and, today, social media have made us all cultural sophisticates, when sophistication is its own form of deadliness. What culture today propagates, whether hordes of zombies or the myth of humankind as random stardust, promptly reaches and sedates the masses. Standing apart from culture is immensely more difficult than it once was, precisely at a time when standing apart may seem most urgent, especially as to attitudes toward death. Don't underestimate the power of culture to influence your attitude toward death. If culture could once make child sacrifice widely accepted, then it likely retains formidable power today.

~

The horrifying call had come in the middle of the night. He had retreated swiftly with the call, pacing back and forth in the basement while talking in hushed and measured tones so as not to disturb his sleeping wife and child. His aging mother had long been suicidal, indeed had fallen in with a younger acquaintance who, likewise suicidal, took his mother to meetings of a society of persons who contemplated and promoted suicide. The mother took up the habit of telephoning her son across the country to announce and re-announce her suicidal interests and intentions, various means that she was considering, and various situational and emotional causes that she discerned for proceeding. Each of her telephone calls set off appropriate alarms, son calling father and other nearby relatives, conferring with mental-health professionals, and trying vainly to counsel mother long distance. This middle-of-the-night call, though, was not from his mother but his father who sobbed repeatedly into the telephone to his son that she once again wanted to die and that all he could do was to hold her to keep her from doing so right then. Son paced back and forth, listening, consoling, and counseling, speaking quietly and caringly but firmly as a parent would speak to help a distraught child regain control. The call finally ended. Mother and father survived another night. Indeed, each died many years later of natural causes, mother only once having tried to take her life, and son only wondering how many other families lived this way.

7

Death and Law

The path of life leads upward for the prudent to keep them from going down to the realm of the dead.

Proverbs 15:24.

Law plays multiple roles around dying and death, as law plays a role at every other stage of life and in every other social endeavor. You are likely familiar with some of those roles, as in the significant debate, legislation, and legal action around physician-assisted death. Who doesn't recall Dr. Jack Kevorkian, convicted of second-degree murder and unlawful delivery of a controlled substance after helping several people commit suicide using medical equipment he installed in his van? Proponents and opponents of the practices deliberately vary in their terms for the practice of physicians hastening death, itself a slippery concept. Proponents call it *death with dignity* and *aid in dying*, while opponents call it *physician-assisted suicide*. The more-neutral term physician-assisted death shouldn't hide the ambiguity of some of the decisions and practices in which physicians and the other care providers whom they direct participate, that hasten rather than delay death. Every decision not to resuscitate, administer antibiotics, pursue a course of chemotherapy, intubate, ventilate, or supply other care and sustenance, may hasten death. To a degree, then, high percentages of patients, their family members, and their care providers engage in decision-making and actions that influence the process of dying and timing of death, including speeding death. Saying so is not to diminish the social, moral, spiritual, economic, and other significance of the issue as to the role that we should play in our own death or the deaths of family members or others about whom we care and as to whom we bear responsibility.

American individualism, the high value that we place on autonomy, self-control, and personal rights of privacy and liberty, certainly should influence our views on the degree to which we should get to decide how and when to die, as should the compassion we hold for one another and the dignity that we wish to preserve. Yet these commitments should not cause us to overlook the consequences to ourselves and others of authorizing others to decide who should die and who should live. The line between assisting another's informed and willing death, and *causing* another's *uninformed* or *unwilling* death, can be difficult to patrol. Societies and communities subtly or not-so-subtly crossing that line seem somehow to first select and cause the deaths of the depressed, different, and disabled. Those societies also point in justification for earlier death to the *cost* of caring for the elderly and disabled, when other societies might instead see care as a *benefit*, both to provider and recipient, indeed even to those who pay for the care. States and nations will continue to experiment with law reforms around the degree to which, actions through which, and circumstances under which physicians may hasten the death of those who wish it for themselves or for others over whose lives they have authorized influence. In those experiments, lawmakers would be wise to heed law professor Joseph Raz's caution, in his article *Death in Our Life*, that one cannot restrict a right to die to narrow circumstances, without widely affecting attitudes about life and death.

Law eventually catches up with those physicians or others who illegally take a living, though also dying, person's life into their own hands, hastening their death. Like America with Jack Kevorkian, England had its own infamous Dr. Death, the general practitioner Harold Shipman who, a special panel found, murdered as many as two hundred fifty of his patients, though convicted of murdering only fifteen. Shipman, who treated patients for nearly three decades, may have been killing patients for most of those three decades, without clear motive. The patients were not uniformly old, suffering, or even ill, and Shipman appeared to gain little if anything from their death at his hands. Although under suspicion for some time due to the large number of patients who died in his practice, authorities eventually charged Shipman only when he forged a patient's will to make himself the beneficiary of about half a million dollars, an act so suspicious that speculation was that Shipman intended his discovery. He committed suicide after a few years in prison. Shipman's story highlights a tension that patients have with their physicians and other care providers. The medical profession certainly wants patients to trust their doctors, but rational persons query whether we can and should do so when dying seems like a progressively greater rather than lesser issue, given increasing medical control over the process. Shipman remains the only English doctor ever convicted of murdering a patient in care.

    Law ensures that patients generally and the terminally ill specifically trust physicians, by restricting physicians from directly hastening a patient's death. Law cannot effectively outlaw suicide. The law is unable to punish those who wish to accomplish suicide and do so. Those who wish to die at their own hand but fail in trying, law and society generally judge worthier of compassion and protection than punishment. Yet law can and generally does outlaw *assisting* suicide. One might think, then, that a physician might simply make painless and efficient means of suicide available to a patient who wished to end his or her life, which was Jack Kevorkian's approach at times. The problem that remains for some patients is that by the time that they confirm their desire and obtain the means from a sympathetic physician, they are already physically unable to invoke the offered means. In those circumstances, patients have made unsuccessful legal challenges to laws against assisted suicide, as medical law professor Hazel Biggs reports in her chapter *Criminalising Carers* in the book *Death Rites and Rights*. Biggs then documents the chilling phenomenon of *death tourism*. Those who wish to die may consider travel to jurisdictions such as Oregon, the Netherlands, and Switzerland that permit assisted suicide. Those jurisdictions, though, with the notable exception of Switzerland, restrict the right to residents. So, Switzerland has been the only recent death-tourism destination, where an organization advocating the right maintains the necessary facility and has participated in thousands of such deaths.

According to legal theorist Foley in her book *The Law of Life and Death,* studies indicate that Oregon residents are increasing their use of the right to medical aid in death. The common means is to obtain a lethal prescription of barbiturates to mix with soft food or drink. An hour after imbibing, the patient is dead. Oregon's law does not require that the patient seeking the prescription be in pain but does require a diagnosis that the patient will die within six months. The law also requires the physician to refer the patient to counseling if judging the patient's judgment impaired. Physicians in fact refer for counseling only a tiny percentage of patients who later choose to imbibe the deadly mix. Patients are also able to go from physician to physician until they find a willing prescriber, without notice to the prescriber that other physicians have refused. A significant percentage of patients using the procedure to end their life are depressed. The law does not require referral for depression. Foley concludes that the Oregon law and a similar one now in place in Washington are not perfect, would benefit from greater procedural protections including court hearings in certain cases especially around coercion by family members, but haven't caused the figurative sky to fall, even while raising troubling issues.

Law, of course, condemns murder, a crime that laws prohibiting assisted suicide have much in mind. The common law defines murder as the unlawful killing of another with malice aforethought, a term of art that encompasses certain intentional killings but also other unintended killings. For example, malice aforethought includes not only intent to kill but also intent to cause serious bodily injury when the action results in death. Malice aforethought also includes the intent to commit certain felonies when the intent results in death. Intentional acts done with depraved indifference to life, when the acts result in death, also satisfy malice aforethought. Modern statutes in many states modify the common-law rules into first-degree murder, second-degree murder, and capital murder, meaning murder for which death is a penalty. First-degree murder includes premeditated killings involving reasoning or deliberation (not an impulse killing) and felony murder, referring to death occurring during certain serious crimes. First-degree murder can also include killing by explosives, torture, poison, or lying in wait, and of an on-duty police officer. Capital murder, defined differently from state to state and not recognized in all states, involves first-degree murder with an aggravating circumstance such as killing of a judge, witness, or on-duty police officer, multiple killings, or killing for hire. One cannot murder a person already dead. Shooters have beaten murder charges on the defense that the person shot was already dead from other causes.

Law does not, on the other hand, ordinarily condemn those who stand idly by while the terminally ill take their own lives, a principle that some jurisdictions feel leaves some room for something like assisted suicide. Caretakers have avoided punishment for having allowed a loved one, for instance, to intentionally overdose on painkillers, as medical law professor Biggs reports in her chapter *Criminalising Carers*. The law has a long history of hesitating to impose duties on those who have not assumed them. One generally has, for instance, no duty to aid or rescue another unless one's own act put them in peril or one stands in some other special relationship to the imperiled. A hospital mental ward or jailer, for example, may owe a duty to prevent the suicide of an insane or severely distraught person confined in their care. But those duties are generally only ones the breach of which may give rise to civil liability, not criminal punishment. Parental abuse and neglect, including reckless disregard of need for basic care, may carry punishment, but standing by while another adult, especially one who is terminally ill, willingly tries to die generally goes unpunished.

The related question that law then addresses is whether one who discovers a person trying to commit suicide has a right to intervene to prevent the suicide. Law professor Antje de Bois-Pedain, in her chapter *Is There a Human Right to Die?* in the book *Death Rites and Rights*, reports that yes, jurisdictions generally permit such intervention, at least outside of the context of a plainly deliberate and obviously well-considered choice by a terminally ill person whom the local jurisdiction accepts has such a right and cause. One may wonder why, if a person in, say, Oregon, the Netherlands, or Switzerland has such a right to commit suicide, may another nonetheless intervene to prevent the act in many cases. The moral and thus also legal justification lies in the uncertainty over whether the person making the attempt has the mental competence to decide and has adequately deliberated over the decision and its consequences. Feel free from a law standpoint, and feel compelled morally, to intervene, the rules may well be, whenever in doubt about the suicide. Yet intervening to prevent a planned and approved suicide at a Swiss right-to-die clinic could result in battery or other criminal charges and civil liability. Privacy is the technical right in which the law grounds these rules preserving some autonomy over one's means and timing of dying. In these legal rules over dying, one finds no rule that compels one to kill another who wishes to die.

The mention immediately above of battery charges or claims against those who provide unwanted care refers to the settled legal principle that one generally controls access to one's own body including the decision whether to provide medical care. A physician must ordinarily have a patient's informed consent to provide care, even life-saving care. A competent adult patient who refuses life-saving medical care ordinarily has the right to do so, making the physician or other medical-care provider who violates the right subject to criminal charge or civil claim for battery. Law grounds this right in the person's dignity, privacy, and autonomy. Individuality includes the right to be let alone. One is less of a person, individual, or human, as we discern humanity, when others have control over one's body. That relatively autonomous control over one's own body, whether to be fit or unfit, tattooed or not, long haired or shorn, pierced or unpierced, blond or brunette, intimate or not, and so forth, helps to define the person as society understands and defines an individual. Law has at times allowed notorious exceptions to this dignitary right, such as when the U.S. Supreme Court approved the forced sterilization of a woman whom care providers had wrongly deemed an imbecile. Yet bad exceptions simply confirm the rule. The informed choice whether to accept life-saving medical care goes right along with those other choices.

Law shows consistent concern to relieve human pain and suffering in death, although not as consistently and effectively as one would prefer to think. The nation and most states do, after all, authorize and carry out capital punishment. Political-science professor Austin Sarat shows in his books *Pain, Death, and the Law* and *Gruesome Spectacles: Botched Executions and America's Death Penalty* that while the U.S. Constitution's Eighth Amendment prohibits cruel-and-unusual punishment, and Supreme Court cases have interpreted that ban to prohibit inflicting more pain than necessary to carry out the sentence of death, the five methods still routinely used do sometimes entail significant pain, and possibly cruelty, before death. Some degree of suffering can still occur under firing squad, hanging, electrocution, gassing, or lethal injection (by far the most-common method), especially when anomalies arise like malfunctioning electrical circuitry or a wrong-measured and not-quite lethal dose. Some, like the murder victim's family members or professionals who must deal with the horrors of the murder scene, show less concern for the perpetrator's suffering under capital punishment. Courts may show as much or more concern for the officials who must witness the execution, and the family members and others who hear about it, as for the executed perpetrator. The modern psyche, Sarat suggests, localizes our empathy in the body of others, even if those others are murderers who have themselves inflicted tortuous pain on their victims, and even when, as law professors Cass Sunstein and Adrian Vermeule cite in *Is Capital Punishment Morally Required?* drawing from a study *Does Capital Punishment Have a Deterrent Effect*, such punishment might save many other lives in deterrent effect. Criticism of the death penalty also includes its seeming randomness, what law professor William Berry calls its *lottery* effect.

    Law faces different issues addressing the death of persons who are in persistent vegetative states. Motor-vehicle accidents, gunshot head wounds, and various diseases leave many American individuals with severe disorders of consciousness, so severe that although the individuals follow sleep-wake patterns and have some reflex response to stimuli, and are clearly *living*, they have little if any awareness of self or environment, or ability for communication or purposeful behavior. A persistent vegetative state differs from a coma, where the individual displays no wakefulness, not even any response to severe stimuli. Some in persistent vegetative state even reach intermittent levels of minimal consciousness. They do not eat or drink, thus requiring intravenous nutrition and hydration, and constant nursing care, without which they would swiftly perish. Most vegetative adults receive that care institutionally, although many vegetative children, representing nearly a third of the vegetative population, receive the care at home. Many live under do-not-resuscitate and no-antibiotics orders. Physicians attempt to distinguish those in a *permanent* vegetative state from merely persistent states that may improve, although the distinctions are more predictive and less reliable than some would think, as a chapter above illustrates.

Law distinguishes physician-assisted-death cases from vegetative-state cases in that the former involve, in theory, only instances where the patient contributes to the decision whether to live or when to die. By contrast, in vegetative-state cases, the patient has no ability to contribute to the decision of how soon to die. Law readily recognizes the right of a person to decide on their own care and, thus, when to die, although law does so only with reasonable safeguards that the person made an informed and reliable decision. Law also readily recognizes the right of a conscious and competent person to document in advanced directive a decision controlling future care and, thus, when to die, even if the authorized absence of care and ensuing death occurs later when the person is no longer conscious and competent. Law wrestles, on the other hand, with whether to allow surrogates to make decisions withholding care and, thus, hastening death, on less-than-reliable evidence of the person's dying wishes. States require clear-and-convincing evidence of the person's wishes, although that evidence need not be in advanced-directive form and may be the testimony of friends and family members, let's hope, not enemies. Some states, though, distinguish between the withdrawal of medical care, generally approved, and the withdrawal of nutrition and hydration, prohibited in those states.

Implicit in these laws is our desire to respect the wishes of the dying not to feel pain in death. Law professor Shai Lavi writes in his chapter *The Problem of Pain and the Right to Die* in the book *Pain, Death and the Law* that Western society has developed an extraordinary intolerance for pain even in, and especially in, death.

Surveys show that the primary reason persons claim a right to die is to avoid pain or even fear of pain. Lavi notes the mistaken attribution of the emergence of a powerful desire to avoid pain, so powerful as to have sufferers seek the ultimate remedy in death, to technological advances that have kept sufferers alive, even painfully alive, much longer. To some, the irony of those medical advances may be that more people today die a slow and painful death. Yet Lavi suggests the inaccuracy of that attribution. Medicine manages pain far better than it once did, even for those whose lives medicine successfully prolongs. Lavi also notes that some attribute extreme pain avoidance to the development of modern sensitivities, another attribution that he rejects. Lavi instead sees the emergence of humane ways to hasten death as related to the intense modern desire to avoid pain in death. Pain in death is not any greater today, and we are no more sensitive to it. Rather, Lavi surmises, the availability of euthanasia and the advance of modern medicine together encourage us to perceive pain in death differently. Pain in death seems to us senseless rather than natural, necessary, and expected, or even graduated and measured. Thus, Lavi concludes, the illusory psychological goal of painlessness now supplants the sanctity of life.

Lavi, though, shares another significant insight having to do with pain at death and how our conception of it affects our treatment of the dying including our own hopes, plans, and directives for death. Pain is personal, sensual, and subjective. Although we treat pain as an epistemological problem (a problem of knowledge), to the contrary no one *knows* another's pain because each of us, more tolerant or less, feels pain sensually and subjectively while also interpreting that pain in differing psychological, experiential, social, and spiritual terms. Yet as modern attitudes toward capital punishment (already mentioned above) also show, when the question comes to how we treat pain in a person dying slowly of natural causes, the knowledge of another's pain becomes communal property, shared among those who care for the dying subject, affecting care decisions and related public policy. No one really knows your pain or my pain, but we nonetheless share one another's pain in a sort of intersubjective fashion. Knowledge of the pain of a dying father or mother thus becomes the shared pain of a living daughter or son, not to mention care providers, guardians, probate judges, and policy makers. Technological and medical advances make pain seem senseless, breaching the sanctity of life and turning pain from a personal crucible into a communal epistemological problem, addressed through such approved methods as terminal sedation and withdrawal of treatment, life support, and even sustenance. Pain no longer has any place in modern society, not even as a rite of passage accompanying the living who lay dying. Norms of dying increasingly prefer death to pain.

The living, though, we sometimes mistakenly report as dead, as Mark Twain famously quipped. Law generally discourages negligent transmission of death notices by holding the careless communicator liable for the surviving loved one's emotional distress. Physicians, medical examiners, hospital officials, law-enforcement officers, funeral-home directors, and others who observe and report on death, all of them sensitive and well-meaning, sometimes get wrong the decedent's identity. You know how things work: if it can go wrong, then at some point it will go wrong. So, one gets the knock on the door or telephone ring in the middle of the night, bearing the awful news of a child's or spouse's traumatic highway or air-crash death. But then, a few horrible hours later, the child or spouse walks in. Overwhelming grief turns instantly to overwhelming relief, which soon turns to anger at the careless communication. Law usually does not hold one liable for distressing another, careless or not, unless the carelessness first produces some physical impact. Yet when the question comes to telling another that their loved one is dead, law makes an exception. Law demands care when announcing another's death.

Law necessarily also has something to say about just what death *is*, meaning just when it occurs. Recall the discussion above about medical definitions of death, including the move from cardiopulmonary standards to brain-death standards. Law, in the form of a uniform act adopted in the great majority of U.S. states, continues to accept both definitions of death. You can imagine the significance. No physician or other medical-care provider or emergency technician wants to face homicide prosecution relating to treatment of, or failure or refusal to treat, persons whom they consider, but others might not consider, dead, whether for organ-donor purposes or otherwise. The law's dual definition of death, including its associated dead-donor rule requiring medical declaration of death before any organ harvesting occurs, facilitates organ transplants. The concern of *living* and unwilling or unknowing donors may sound alarming, and it should. Other countries face substantial and just public and political condemnation for harvesting organs of unwilling prisoners and religious minorities, causing their death.

Drawing from English common law, U.S. law has in the past recognized a concept of *civil death* in which those convicted of serious crimes lost law's protections, becoming a sort of legal persona non grata. While civil death did not allow another to kill the convicted criminal, whether to harvest organs or for other purposes, the convicted criminal might not be able to move, travel, marry, work, vote, own property, hold licenses, or even be physically in certain places. Law professor Gabriel Chin points out in his article *The New Civil Death* that some present collateral consequences of conviction, like offender registries and housing restrictions, operate like a modern form of civil death. The challenge of repatriating to distant homelands incarcerated enemy combatants whom those homelands refuse to accept creates a more-dire, even if deserved, form of modern civil death. Legal limbo, while not organic death, can nonetheless be its own form of hell.

Oddly, though necessarily, law also protects the dead from the living. We find today much use for the living organs and dead bodies of the departed, for transplant, law-enforcement medical forensics, medical and epidemiological research, medical training, and other study. Law prohibits the living or their survivors who control the disposition of their dead bodies from selling bodies or body parts. We don't want people selling off their kidneys, even if we do want people consenting to donate. Others clearly profit from the services that they perform and products that they sell related to organ harvesting, cadaver sale, and other beneficial trade in the bodies of the dead, as is appropriate in a market-based society and economy. Yet when those market actors get too hasty or careless, and dispose of bodies and body parts that they shouldn't, law provides the family members various remedies. I once represented a couple whose young son had suddenly died. The hospital compounded the shock by promptly removing their dead son's eyes, parts of which the hospital could transplant into living patients. The parents might, had they thought about it, have authorized the invasion, but they hadn't even seen the body of their dead son yet. Law often provides a civil remedy in the form of compensation for the negligent mishandling of a corpse.

Criminal laws in various jurisdictions prohibit others from interfering with the work of a coroner in preserving and examining the dead body or interfering with the burial of human remains. Criminal laws also punish for desecrating the memorials of the interred. Communities may show special outrage against those, perhaps youth vandals, who topple over headstones and spray paint monuments. Criminal or civil law may also discourage and punish as a public nuisance, transgressive displays of human remains. Law takes care to preserve a degree of order and even sacredness around the rituals with which we treat the departed. Civil-liability laws not only compensate for losses but also discourage the carelessness that causes them. All U.S. states have wrongful-death acts that permit the living to recover for the decedent's death, when caused by another's tortious act, typically negligence in the operation of a motor vehicle but in other ways, too. Studies suggest that liability laws do deter some deaths, although law professors Paul Rubin and Joanna Shepherd show in their article *Tort Reform and Accidental Death* that the effects are more complex and that various reforms of those laws can either increase or decrease deaths.

To carry out those wrongful-death acts, law must measure the loss attendant on death, and not just as a public policy matter, as for instance when economist Kip Viscusi's study *The Value of Life* places a seven-million-dollar value on a U.S. resident's life. Wrongful-death acts vary widely in how they measure the loss of a life. Odd as it may seem, some states have the jury measure the dead person's own loss including not only lost earned income but also lost enjoyment of life. Some of those states reduce the dead person's income loss for personal consumption that the death saved. Other states measure the loss to surviving family members, sometimes including not only the loss of financial support but also the loss of love, society, and companionship. States also differ on which family members get to recover loss, some states restricting recovery to spouses and dependent children, while other states grant recovery to spouse, parents, grandparents, siblings, children, grandchildren, and other lineal descendants, even if in no sense dependent. Lawyers also differ on how they prove these losses, certainly through the testimony of close family members and acquaintances but also through education records, employment records, photo albums, cards, letters, memorial bulletins, funeral registers, and all manner of other exhibits.

In these wrongful-death cases, law also awards money damages for the decedent's conscious pain and suffering just before death, if in fact the decedent saw death coming. Law recognizes that anticipating one's imminent traumatic death is a special kind of loss, never mind for a moment that one will momentarily be dead anyway. In one of the air-crash cases in which I represented the estate of a person killed in the accident, I met a lawyer who traveled the world representing the families of air-crash victims. In some of his cases, the decedents had been aboard airliners that plummeted out of the sky, plainly alerting all aboard of their imminent demise. In others of his cases, the decedents had survived the crash only to slowly drown, trapped in the sinking remains of the fuselage, or slowly choke and burn to death, trapped in the fuselage's wreckage. How, I asked him, did juries tend to measure that fear-of-horrible-death loss? His answer was a few thousand dollars, possibly as much as ten-thousand dollars, per second, maybe not as much as one would think in a theoretical market for pain. You and I would probably pay much more than that amount to avoid such a death, if we could.

The law, though, prohibits trial lawyers from making what it calls the *Golden-Rule argument.* One must not in closing argument encourage jurors to place themselves in the position of the decedent or injured plaintiff, when measuring the value of their suffering. The argument is, for one, too powerful. Imagine, for instance, that *you* are the one drowning in the crashed jetliner. Your willingness to make a substantial jury award may have just increased significantly.

We find it easier to judge the fear, pain, and suffering of others than we find judging our own pain. The argument, though, may also be misleading. Jurors are not the decedent or injured plaintiff. Their experience of serious injury or impending death would inevitably be at least a little different from the experience of the one who suffered it. Trial lawyers must thus find ways to communicate that unique loss in its peculiar context, without playing directly on juror sympathy. The above example of the impending air cash illustrates one way that trial lawyers help jurors measure the decedent's suffering, which is to divide it into days, hours, minutes, or even seconds. If one has only twenty-three seconds to live in an airliner tumbling high out of the sky toward the middle of the frigid ocean, then each second of life may hold its own value, whether one measures that value in intense prayers and poignant memories passing swiftly through the mind or, conversely, sheer terror.

I represented several whose loved ones had died suddenly and unexpectedly through the carelessness of another, such as in a motor-vehicle accident or plane crash, but also sometimes through the wrongdoer's deliberate act. In one case, the father of a woman's child had murdered the woman over a custody dispute. In another case, a drunken man had walked out of a bar, shooting his revolver at anything and nothing, striking my client estate's decedent in the head. In another case, a helicopter's engine had suddenly quit, the helicopter falling 500 feet out of the sky, killing its four occupants. In another case, a drill press had shot a chunk of lead into my client estate's decedent's chest. In a more-typical case, a drunken driver had let her vehicle wander from the road into a tree, killing her passenger. The legal proceedings arising out of these horrible events gave voice to the family members' grief. We collected the stories, photographs, correspondence, and other memories of what the decedent's life had meant, presenting that evidence for the other side to take account. The cases invariably drew other-worldly quality to them from the decedent's absence. Plenty of legal cases depict substantial loss, but the loss in a wrongful-death case is unique, in a category to itself.

Law struggles with how to treat the question of suicide, in wrongful-death cases. Sometimes, one party's negligence may cause the serious injury of another, so serious that the injured person becomes depressed and suicidal. Civil-liability laws compensate the injured person for mental and emotional distress, including depression. But when the depressed person then commits suicide, must the negligent party who caused the injury and depression also pay for the death? Death at one's own hands seems different from injury suffered at the hands of another. Traditionally, law refuses to compensate for the suicide unless due to organic brain injury and irresistible impulse. Diagnosis of organic brain injury serves the purpose of removing much of the question of what caused the depression and suicide. Irresistible impulse, though, is not a medical term but only a nebulous legal term, used to distinguish volitional suicides for which no one should pay from suicides compelled by the injury, for which the negligent party causing the injury should pay. One odd case that Foley reports involved a woman whom medical-care providers mistakenly informed had a deadly cancerous brain tumor. She had no tumor but nonetheless committed suicide for having reasonably believed that she did. Her husband successfully maintained a civil action for damages against the medical-care providers, proving that their negligence created an irresistible impulse for her suicide. More common cases involve simple motor-vehicle accidents causing such serious injury that the depressed victim commits suicide.

How much these legal issues should or do influence us in how we think about and countenance death is hard to know. I am a lawyer, and so I take greater interest in legislation and legal proceedings than the non-lawyer might take, even having reviewed the widely distributed, tongue-in-cheek law-review article on *Death and Taxes and Zombies*. As law professor Susan Wolf wrote in her article *Pragmatism in the Face of Death*, lawyers prefer to work within the field of rights, documentation, and arm's length transactions. Yet I also find that I don't need to draw personal conclusions about death and dying from legal debates, which tend to inform but don't necessarily convince. Other beliefs, commitments, experiences, and understandings tend so strongly to influence one's view of how law should treat death that law itself is not necessarily an effective influence. Law does, however, necessarily moderate these debates. It must. We must have rules. As cultural anthropologist Donald

Joralemon concludes, death is clearly not just a medical event but also a social and legal event, as well as a consultative process. Each regime has its place in helping us countenance death, whether our own death, the death of a loved one, or the death of a stranger or many strangers. These and other death regimes change constantly, influencing one another as they do, and likely also influencing subtly how any one of us thinks of and prepares for, or refuses to prepare for, our own death.

~

The lawyer hadn't met his client until now, for her deposition. To that point, the case had been all pleadings, discovery requests, and exchanges of records and information, documenting the road worker's sudden death. The lawyer suspected that the deposition would be especially hard for his client. Indeed, in a way, he hoped so. She had somehow driven at nearly full speed straight into the road worker who had been signaling her with one of those hand signs to stop. The worker, of course, had died instantly, his head striking and shattering her vehicle's windshield. The lawyer, experienced in handling death cases, already had a good sense of the loss. What the lawyer couldn't quite imagine, though, was how his own client was reaching terms with having been the awful cause of the worker's death. He knew from police reports that she professed having no memory of the event. He only hoped that the deposition would be another step in her reaching those terms with having been the horribly unfortunate and sadly unwitting harbinger of a happy man's death.

8

Death and History

The realm of the dead below is all astir
to meet you at your coming;
it rouses the spirits of the departed to greet you—
... maggots are spread out beneath you
and worms cover you.

Isaiah 14:9-11.

Philosopher Paul Fairfield in *Death: A Philosophical Inquiry* writes that today's scientific and technological worldview does little to help us think about death in any way other than superficially, and that we must therefore instead turn for that help to the ancients. Some societies, past or present, may deal better, or least more openly, with death than others, although making judgments across time and culture is difficult, and one finds it too easy to condemn the present and local in favor of the distant and past. Popular culture today makes much, for instance, in museum shows, literature, television, music, and film, of the ancient Egyptians' mummies and tombs. The Great Pyramids are enduring symbols of the ancient society's spectacular treatment of the royal dead. The effort was to preserve the body as the person's spiritual home. Commoners got shallow graves in which the dry desert air sometimes did the preservation trick. Royalty got the elaborate tombs. In both cases, families made the effort to preserve the body or an appearance of the body, such as with masks, wigs, and image-decorated sarcophagi, along with perfumes, food, and other comforts for the afterlife trip.

In their rituals, the ancient Egyptians were in a broad sense heirs to what archaeologists say to have been thousands or tens of thousands of years of humans caring for their dead. Caring for the dead, so closely tied to caring about death, may be one of those attributes that makes us human. Historian William Spellman in his book *A Brief History of Death* finds little pattern to how humans have treated their dead. The pattern, if any, is simply one of continuous engagement with our dead since antiquity. Stone, some suggest, humans used for sepulchers before use for housing. Tombs, others similarly speculate, may have been the first human architecture. Yet histories of death, like Spellman's or French historian Philippe Aries' *The Hour of Our Death*, tend to show not how much but how little history can tell us with confidence about what the primitive and ancients truly thought of death. Spellman, for instance, senses a shift in ancient times from clan cohesion around death to individual relationship with God, while Aries sees a similar shift from death-as-other to death-as-self but not occurring until the Renaissance. We have no sure way of knowing that either is true. Ancients and their primitive forebears may have been just as individually concerned as moderns about the journey of their souls in death. Friends and relatives leave the oddest comforts, including toys, sports gear, clothing, jewelry, and food and drink, at fresh gravesites today, much as archaeologists find equivalent comforts in the ancient tombs. Do these gifts really signify what we project onto them?

The ancient Greeks differed about death, some like Plato and Hippocrates in degrees agreeing with the Egyptians as to the surviving spirit or soul, while others like Aristotle and Epicurus seeing death as dissolution of body and soul. Greeks and Romans knew, though, that discerning the divide between life and death could be tricky, and that medical conditions of the living could mimic death. Ancient Greek and Roman funeral and burial practices thus tried to ensure that they weren't mistreating the living in disposing of the dead. If cremation was the course, as it was for some in those ancient societies, then first waiting a few days or at least cutting off a finger to watch for any response was a preferred approach. If burial was the plan, then first trying to revive the body with rubbing, warm baths, and ritual name-calling, and again waiting a few days, were wise practices. Ancient Hebrews may have watched for the decomposing abdomen to extend with putrefaction gases before moving the body for burial.

All monitored breathing and heartbeat as indicators of death, but most took precautions not to let observations mislead. Some ancients also kept flowers around the body during these waiting periods, not as today solely to cheer the living but rather then also to perfume the stink of the dead. If putrefaction was the sure way of ensuring that the deceased had in fact departed, then social customs including not only flowers but rubbing the body with myrrh, aloes, and other aromatic gums and spices, and wrapping the body in cloth strips, made much sense. Varied practices like and unlike these, to ensure death while also preparing and preserving the body for burial, cremation, or other disposition, continued through the Middle Ages and into modernity. One widely influential 1772 Mecklenburg decree imposed a three-day wait between declaration of death and burial to ensure, through observation of some degree of decomposition, that society only buried the dead, not the living.

Renaissance interest in anatomy and medicine brought new efforts to acquire bodies for dissection if not yet, as now, organ transplant. Records from the early age tell us of theaters where anatomists dissected bodies of dead persons and live dogs in public performance. That bodies then had a public use for science, medicine, or even performance, created potential for conflict with the previously expressed interests of the deceased and the interests of survivors, a conflict of interests that continues to today. As science and medicine advanced, dissection became a regular part of medical training, increasing demand for dead bodies. A trade, mostly illicit, arose for body snatchers in the dark of night to dig up graves of the just-buried, to deliver the body at high price to the medical schools for dissection. As anatomical knowledge and associated skills advanced, demand arose for autopsies of the dead. Royal decree made the bodies of executed criminals the first to be officially available for dissection and autopsy.

Pursuit of anatomical knowledge didn't only affect the dead but also aided the living. History had long recorded successful resuscitations of the near dead or believed dead, especially victims who had fallen into waterways. Physician and medical professor David Casarett reports, in his book *Shocked: Adventures in Bringing Back the Recently Dead*, that both Amsterdam and London, for their many urban waterways, developed primitive-sounding professions for rescuing and resuscitating the drowned. Rolling the body over a log to expel water from the lungs, rubbing and warming the body, and tickling the throat with a feather to trigger a cough reflex, were rational methods among other more-bizarre practices the resuscitators used to try to restore heartbeat and breathing. While the resuscitators themselves and others' records of their activities reported some remarkable successes, experts today regard many if not all those successes as artifacts for other explanations including showmanship, fraud, and that the purported victim hadn't really drowned at all but was merely a haplessly drunk convenience for the resuscitator's theatric performance.

Medical advances, though, have led to at least a few extraordinary rescues and resuscitations, and not just of the fifteen-to-twenty-minutes-under-water type. Casarett details one instance of an adult skier getting trapped for *eighty minutes* in extremely cold water under river ice. Heroic and extraordinarily fortuitous circumstances, if one can call *fortuitous* anything associated with such a horrific drowning, contributed to the skier's nearly complete recovery, after almost *five hours* without breathing or a heartbeat. The skier's recovery was so complete that she married one of her rescuers, who had been skiing with her that day, and resumed her career as a physician. Casarett cautions, though, that the usual outcome for even relatively brief duration without breathing and heartbeat remains very poor. Resuscitation techniques have improved greatly along with better knowledge of cardiopulmonary management and effects, but any real success still largely depends on initial conditions beyond the care providers' control, like a very cold dying body and very prompt and extraordinary intervention. Casarett instead devotes most of his book to debunking or at least tamping down expectations around the fantastic claims of resuscitators, cryogeneticists, and others placing their trust in suspended animation of the dead or, in the most-bizarre case, their heads, in hopes of future resuscitation.

Cardiologist and medical professor Warraich, in his book *Modern Death*, records a different kind of *autoresuscitation* that in his account has both an ancient history and modern twist. Autoresuscitation involves the declared decedent's heart restarting on its own rather than with medical intervention. The phenomenon presumably occurs naturally, and perhaps relatively often, before medical intervention. Hearts stop beating due to shock of one kind or another disrupting and ending the pattern of electrical stimulus of the heart muscle. Some physiological trigger, though, can, even without artificial intervention, cause electrical signals to resume and gradually increase and organize until the heart beats once again. The issue is that the phenomenon has also occurred *after* medical intervention, in other words after emergency medical personnel have given up the patient for dead. Warraich calls it the Lazarus effect after the Bible account of Jesus calling his several-days-dead friend out of the tomb. The biblical allusion may not be helpful. No modern account records anyone doing anything like calling a several-days-dead patient into autoresuscitation. Instead, the modern twist is that the contemporary brain-death standard has increased the number of early declarations of death, well before putrefaction and even before cardiopulmonary failure, while arguably decreasing the reliability of declarations of death, given that they depend on ascertaining the absence of brain waves only indirectly. Warraich opines that autoresuscitations probably go underreported because of the embarrassment and legal consequences of giving up the living for dead.

Recent history, though, has given the modern mind far clearer images, symbols, and markers of death, in its world wars, death marches, concentration camps, killing fields, and genocides. Who, when surveying a brief history of death, cannot think of the twentieth century's two world wars, killing forty million and fifty-eight million respectively, taking common estimates? World War II alone extinguished the lives of about three percent of all those then living worldwide. The two World Wars of the twentieth century, making that century the bloodiest overall, find a rival in China's Taiping Civil War of the mid 1800's, killing somewhere around forty-four million. By contrast, only about a half million died in the U.S. Civil War, which though still horrific doesn't even make the long list of bloodiest wars. Various long-term conquests, such as the Mongols' century-long conquest of Eurasia, China's century-long Three Kingdom's War, and China's half-century Qing Dynasty conquest of the Ming Dynasty, each killed tens of millions, as may have the two-century conquest of Native Americans, depending on widely varying population estimates and the degree to which one counts deaths by displacement and disease.

To the Western mind, though, World War I's trench-and-gas warfare and World War II's death marches, death trains, gas chambers, and concentration camps capture the extraordinary horrors of death amid war. Holocaust survivor Elie Wiesel's book *Night* chronicles the utter loss of hope that so many suffered in Auschwitz, Buchenwald, and other camps, as they watched family members worked or beaten to death or led away to the gas chambers, hope that Wiesel miraculously recovered in his next works *Dawn* and *Day*. One must turn to art, film, and literature, and to faith, to recover hope and humanity out of such depths of horror and chaos. Art helped win the war with its heroic poster images and film propaganda and then helped humanity recover from the war with revealing stories of courage, resistance, and suffering, even as art had also led the world into war, for example with German film director Leni Riefenstahl's classic Nazi propaganda films *Triumph of the Will* and *Olympia*. Art now has the task of helping us remember the horrible lessons of Auschwitz, treating those lessons of the peril of the absolute sovereignty of the nation-state over the individual, as death's extraordinarily expensive gift. As if to prove that humankind still had lessons to learn after two world wars, the twentieth century's onslaught continued with Cambodian killing fields and Bosnian and Rwandan genocides. Syrian civil war, massive refugee movements, and deadly jihadist atrocities question whether the twenty-first century will be significantly different in the numbers and terror in which people will die violent war deaths.

War's horror lies not entirely in combatant deaths but also in civilian non-combatant deaths that, surprisingly or not, tend to outnumber combatant deaths. Ethics scholar Lloyd Steffen, in his chapter *Stop the Killing* in the book *Unequal Before Death*, reports that 30 million civilians died among World War II's 55 million deaths. Civilians die to war's artillery and bombs, just like the targeted soldiers do. Hiroshima lost 70,000 to the atomic bomb's blast but another 200,000 in the following years from radiation poisoning. Citizen non-combatants also die in extraordinary numbers from war's infrastructure damage and lawless disorder. The Iraq War may have killed around 100,000 directly but another half million to one million from hunger, disease, exposure, lack of medical care, and similar causes due to social, medical, financial, and legal disruption. While Steffen repeats the conventions that nations must avoid war when possible and when waging war must treat non-soldier citizens as protected non-combatants, his figures purposely challenge the possibility of achieving the latter convention.

Deaths in large numbers, under both natural and human causes, will doubtless continue to remind us of our mortality. The anthology *Making Sense of Death, Dying and Bereavement* collects stories of recent traumatic deaths. Two stories recount the Indian Ocean tsunami that killed well over 200,000. Another story recounts a football-stadium crowd crushing and killing dozens, the author physician walking helplessly among the dead. Another story mentions ferry and riverboat sinkings, air crashes, building fires, mass shootings, and terrorist attacks and bombings. Families of victims would wonder why no one tried in many of these events to preserve individual belongings, to rescue some small bit of humanity out of the carnage. An official whose job entailed exactly that difficult task tells her own story of returning tens of thousands of bits of property to the families of the dead.

Accounts tell how those family members at times feel howling pain while at other times suffer numb shock, all the time struggling to believe the awful event real. Mundane activities, the things that once gave life some shape, lose all meaning. Survivors would feel different from, and to degrees ignored by, anyone who had not experienced the event by also having lost a family member. Some survivors fixate on video and press reports of their event simply to try to grasp that the event, so unimaginable, was in fact real. Flashbacks, panic attacks, glazed feelings, and feelings of isolation soon follow. Some survivors simply freeze at times, unable to move. Post-disaster effects are not simply psychological and emotional.

Econometrics professors Jesse Keith Antilla-Hughes and Solomon Hsiang report in their study *Destruction, Disinvestment, and Death* that post-disaster losses, including infant mortality, from such as a West Pacific typhoon may exceed direct losses and deaths by a ratio of fifteen to one. The aftermath of natural catastrophe may be far deadlier than the catastrophe itself.

Philosophy lecturer Belshaw, in his book *Annihilation*, raises a good question, one that may inform how one thinks of death, whether it is worse for more to die than for less to die. The obvious answer, yes, may not be the most sensitive or accurate answer in any one instance of multiple deaths. Recall discussion above that we might reasonably consider it worse to die young than to die old because of the loss of expected life, even countenancing Epicurus's objection that the one who dies would not be conscious to experience the loss. Yet when several persons die at once, some may be young and others may be old. Some may suffer greater loss in dying than others lose, Epicurean objections aside. One young decedent may lose more than two elderly decedents. Additionally, Belshaw suggests that if several must die, then their opportunity for survival may affect the evil of their deaths. Whether in the sinking of the Titanic or the defense of the Alamo, how bad death is may depend on its fairness, including the decedent's ability to affect the outcome, such as to choose whether to live at the expense of other lives or to die saving others. The cost or loss of death, and corollary value of life, even in numbers terms, is not so simple.

History gives little clear calculus, though, as to how to predict, value, and adjust for the deaths of few or of many, in wars, famines, purges, and revolutions, and their displacements. Death is not always in avoidance but sometimes in choice and commitment, as when a nation divides for citizens to take up arms against one another in civil war, or when a nation goes to war in defense of its people, lands, and liberties. Looking back, history tends to give us relatively clear narratives on the choice to commit many to their deaths. One war was to free an emerging nation of its extortionate colonizer, while another was to rid the land of slavery, and others to wrest world peace from fascist and imperialist enemies. Looking back, the narratives seem so simple, even as we suspect that the narratives may be as much myth-making as fact. Yet history does not project us forward nearly so well. The book *Beyond Biopolitics: The Governance of Life and Death* gives some hints at power dynamics that may lay just beneath the surface of what societies and nations profess to achieve when they go to war or otherwise commit their resources in ways that will surely bring about many deaths. When we commit one another to die, let us hope that we do so for just, clear, and lasting ends.

Studies of death do reveal demographic patterns and social stratifications, implicating justice issues. Take the question of age. Few might say that to expect the old to die more often than the young, and the young less often than the old, would raise issues of unwarranted discrimination. Yet public policy must allocate resources among segments of the population. Qualifying for Medicare to pay without practical limit for their progressively greater healthcare needs, the elderly population consumes significantly more healthcare than any other segment of the U.S. population, straining federal and state budgets. Elderly persons have also gained greater ability to pay for care that government programs do not provide. Christina Staudt, in the introduction to her book *Unequal Before Death*, reports a huge shift over the past fifty years in U.S. poverty rates. In 1960, more than one third of U.S. elderly lived in poverty, whereas today less than ten percent do, while child-poverty rates have remained nearly stable over the same period at twenty to twenty-five percent. More young are poor today than old are poor in part because of public policy.

Poverty rates and government decisions to allocate funds to certain programs affect mortality. Staudt gives as examples enormous improvements in infant mortality rates that Botswana made, in just one decade lowering the rate from 76 per 1,000 live births to just 12 per 1,000 live births, while rates in neighboring Namibia, without similar programs and funding, declined only from 56 to 45 per 1,000 live births. Infant mortality is a huge worldwide concern, with 25,000 children dying daily of preventable diseases as to which families in developed nations face little concern. Poverty affects not just infant mortality but also death rates up to age forty-five. Scholars disagree on how *much* poverty affects death rates.

Staudt reports one study holding that 4.5% of all U.S. deaths are due to poverty, low education, or other social disadvantage, while another scholar suggests that as many as 25% of premature U.S. deaths under age sixty-five are the result of income disparities.

Not just age but also ethnicity affects mortality rates, and not always in the way that one might suspect. Yes, Staudt reports, African-American men have a life expectancy more than fifteen years shorter than Asian-American men. The differences are also regional. Southern African-American women have a life expectancy nearly thirteen years shorter than southern Asian-American women. The disadvantages also include causes of death, with African Americans about six times as likely to die from assault as Caucasian Americans, and Asian Americans about half as likely. Income and insurance are factors affecting these differences in mortality along ethnic lines, but so, too, is the proximity of certain populations to healthcare facilities. Evidently, the closer one lives to the hospital or clinic, the healthier and longer one may live. Yet Caucasian Americans, while generally faring better than their African-American counterparts, have higher morbidity and premature-death rates once widowed than do their African-American widowed counterparts. Anthropologist Margaret Souza, in her chapter *When the Poor Get More* in Staudt's book *Unequal Before Death*, also reports some evidence for the anomaly that U.S. poor get more medical care at end of life than do the rich who have greater control over the course of dying.

Economist Amartya Sen brought to light another remarkable modern mortality phenomenon implicating justice issues. Sen estimates that since around the 1980s, 100 million women have gone missing, mostly from Asia, North Africa, and the Middle East, where many countries now have a significant population imbalance favoring men. Sen and other researchers attribute the phenomenon to sex-selective abortions, female infanticide, and poor food and medicine for girls in countries whose policies and cultures favor male children for their economic productivity. Other researchers also blame sexually transmitted diseases, female abductions, and mortality related to pregnancy and childbirth, but still leaving preference for male children as the primary cause. Various studies have challenged Sen's 100-million figure, and the actual number may be significantly below that estimate but still many tens of millions.

The history and demography of death can thus broadly inform one about the subjects of life, dying, and death. The compelling history, though, remains that death is certain. And whatever we learn about death from looking across lands and generations, death remains peculiarly individual and personal. We may know from history more about when, where, how, and why we die, making the history of death a worthwhile subject, but history won't necessarily teach us how to approach and countenance our own death in our daily course of living and dying. Although history has much to say about all things including death, we need to look elsewhere for that ultimate counsel.

~

His father had died just an hour ago, son holding father's hand as father breathed his last breath. The nurse had called for the clinician to make the official pronouncement, which had taken just spare minutes. Nurse and clinician left the son with the father's dead body to reflect for a respectable time. Son prayed, surely, although realizing as he did so that the time for supplication had passed and that prayer should somehow instead be in thanksgiving. Son's thoughts then turned to his mother, whom an attendant kindly agreed to wake from her afternoon nap and wheel into the nursing home's nearby sunroom. Son first sat silently with mother for a few minutes, letting her compose what little she could of her hopelessly scattered thoughts, dementia having long ago stolen her recognition and reason. Mother's kind smile suggested that she might have briefly recognized her son. So, son began, gently and indirectly at first, but soon as clearly as he could muster, to tell his mother that her husband of nearly sixty years had just died. Another flicker of recognition passed across mother's serene face, possibly with a moment's sadness. Mother began to speak, which she almost never any longer did. Her words, though individually recognizable, would if taken together have been utter nonsense to anyone but her son. Yet her son could just perceive in his mother's fancifully disjointed references that she knew the moment's meaning, even that she was both glad and sad that her husband's present journey had ended. Son hugged mother as her words trailed off into nonsensical phrases, the moment's profound meaning swiftly fading to the return of an oddly comforting dementia. The two sat silently together in the afternoon sun.

9

Death and Philosophy

> *People of Athens! I see that in every way you are very religious. For as I walked around and looked carefully at your objects of worship, I even found an altar with this inscription: to an unknown god. So you are ignorant of the very thing you worship—and this is what I am going to proclaim to you.*
>
> Acts 17:22-23.

Philosophers, in their own inimitable ways, make uneven contributions to our ability to face death meaningfully, some contributions profound and others seeming silly. Take first an example of the silly-seeming. French Renaissance skeptic Michel de Montaigne in his essay *To Study Philosophy Is to Learn to Die* wrote that lamenting that we die is as foolish as lamenting that we did not live a hundred years earlier. When we project the lost enjoyment of life that death brings, we quite naturally only do so for experience lost *after* death rather than for things that we might have experienced and enjoyed if we had been born *sooner*. Death, after all, is the difference. Death has nothing to do with not having been born sooner, and only a foolish philosopher would argue so, or so it surely seems.

Yet the question of non-existence before birth and non-existence (if that is your view of one's situation) after death does raise what philosophy professor James Warren, author of the book *Facing Death*, identifies as a *symmetry problem*, in a chapter by that name in the *Cambridge Companion*. If the absence of life after death is a loss, then why isn't the absence of life before birth also a loss? Probably, few of us have decried not having been born earlier to enjoy or make a mark on an earlier time, although then again, some persons do seem peculiarly fitted for an earlier age. The point, though, is to examine the attitude that we hold toward death representing the possibility of nonexistence. And what reason suggests is indeed that we sense loss in the possibility of future nonexistence exactly because such loss would represent deprivation. We feel entitled to a certain life, to continued life, even if we have no basis for claiming entitlement to an earlier life, to having been born sooner or in some sense having always existed in the mind of the Creator.

Philosophy seems highly abstract, when death, as we face and experience it, surely seems concrete and certain. In that vein, philosophy professor John Martin Fischer, in his chapter *Mortal Harm* in the same book, studies what he identifies as the Epicurean's *experience requirement*. How, the Epicurean asks, can the condition of being dead be a bad thing when one doesn't experience it? In that view, being dead must instead be neutral. Think even of some unknown harm that goes on behind your back while you are still living, such as a person ruining your reputation with defamation. If you never find out, then you may not have suffered any harm. Maybe being dead is like the harm that you never discover. Think then of the wise and sophisticated adult whose sudden brain injury makes the person like a little child. If the formerly wise and sophisticated person is just as happy as a little child, then maybe the person has suffered no harm. Yet most of us, like Fischer, would disagree. We instead perceive the loss of a better life, in the defamation case a life of better reputation, in the brain-injury case the life of a wise adult, and in the case of too-early of a death the loss of the life that the person who died would have lived. So, experience isn't everything. Perception also counts for something.

Consider a far more significant symmetry problem that death raises. I have known others who, like me, have had good reason to believe that our mothers never would have borne us if abortion had been legal when our parents conceived us. One was a wonderful man whose teenage mother gave him and his twin brother up for adoption at birth. They were not adopted, and Boys Town raised them instead. The question, though, is whether either would have suffered loss if their mother had aborted them rather than borne them and given to Boys Town to raise. Most of us who have survived the womb to live a good life would likely attest that yes, *we* would have suffered great loss if our mothers had not carried us to term. Yet if our mothers had not carried us to term, we would not be here to say so. Our prospective lives might then, depending on how one looks at it in a question that sharply divides society right now, only have been the potential of life lost rather than that of taking back what one has already gained. Tens of millions of aborted Americans are not here to say so, which either makes an enormous difference or no difference at all. Have they lost, or have we lost, because of their death? In the maw of that question, we find one awfully difficult issue.

Proponents of abortion rights must generally construe the fact of birth as critical to the born person's own right at a chance to live a full life. For such proponents, birth makes a difference in whether one sees a premature death as a person's loss. Once born, then yes, a premature death is the dead person's loss, but if not born, then no, death before birth is no loss. A few abortion proponents, university bioethicist Peter Singer has suggested, might extend the killing right beyond birth until the child reaches some more-advanced point of sentience. Yet thankfully, law's presumption so far remains that the person whom someone kills at age one, ten, or twenty years, suffers a greater loss than the not-yet-born child, indeed a loss against which society protects by defining the killing act as murder. Abortion proponents do not generally afford the same sense of loss to the unborn child. In their view, potential counts only from birth, viability, or some other point. Abortion opponents hold the opposite that the unborn child loses life, as do those who would have welcomed the child. So, how nonexistence affects our view of death is not quite so simple as thinking of the old person dying of natural causes or even the young person dying in a motor-vehicle accident.

Posthumous benefit and harm are other close questions death raises. For instance, do we have anything to gain, once having died, in our surviving relatives treating our estate as we directed? Law and society presume so, going to great lengths to see that courts probate estates as the decedent directs. Or do we instead follow the dead person's wishes solely for the benefit of the living? Do we gain if, posthumously, others recognize some good that we did while alive or, conversely, others spoil our memory with false allegations? Philosophy professor Simon Keller, in a chapter *Posthumous Harm* in the *Cambridge Companion* suggests that the answer is, again, a little subtler than one might think. How we should think about posthumous benefit or harm may depend on how we measure a good life, whether by the pleasures enjoyed or objectives obtained, including in the latter case a good reputation. The question's other significance is that how we think of posthumous benefit or harm influences how we think and act today, while alive. If we wish to leave a legacy, to create something that outlasts our own lives, then clearly, posthumous benefit or harm matters.

Thus, how much should one sacrifice today to have others benefit tomorrow and have those others remember one posthumously for the sacrifice one made for their good? This question of legacy goes two ways, too. Legacy doesn't merely depend on a person's actions before death. Legacy also depends on the posthumous actions of the persons for whom the decedent acted. Think of it: a patriarch or matriarch may sacrifice much so that children would benefit. Yet if the children all decide to be scoundrels, wasting the benefits, the legacy likely suffers with it. On the other hand, should any of us live in ways that to any significant degree constrain the choices of those who survive us, even if the constraints involve what most would think of as positive legacy? Even as we live, anticipating death, we can also make, and perhaps should make, judgments of posthumous harm and benefit, and posthumous effects, no matter how we conceive of ourselves, existent or nonexistent, after death.

Philosophers tend toward the conclusion that death imbues life or at least that we *ought* to think about death while living, as philosophy professor Paul Fairfield writes in *Death: A Philosophical Inquiry*. Death invokes soul-searching about the meaning of one's life, to the point that one can cast aside life's trivialities to embrace life's essentials. The turning within that contemplating death requires becomes a source of creative and authentic engagement with the world, helping us replace superficial activities with actions having unique personal identity. In the first existential philosopher Soren Kierkegaard's way of putting it, death helps us accomplish a liberating personal appropriation of meaning. Thinking about death makes one define one's self as fully human. To German philosopher Martin Heidegger, death is the coloring or atmosphere of life, and to French Renaissance philosopher Michel de Montaigne the continuous work of life.

Indeed, Fairfield credits Heidegger with the most-important modern philosophical statement about death that life is a being-toward-death, a sort of foreshadowing of death and thus a becoming alive because of death. Paolo Palladino, in *Biopolitics and the Philosophy of Death*, notes how Heidegger, in his *Being and Time*, reconstructed philosophy around a reflective view of death as immanent within life, existence and consciousness arising out of that living knowledge of impending death. To philosopher Friedrich Nietzsche, death should be a consummation of and fitting end to life, spurring fulfillment of promise to the living. We should not adopt mordant preoccupation with death but should also not ignore that its bounds help us to choose our actions to define who we are. Think of life without death. Would your life have any of the arc or trajectory, urgency or poignancy, passion or purpose that it currently has, if you projected it no end? Fairfield credits philosopher and sociologist Herbert Marcuse, in Fairfield's work *The Ideology of Death*, with the thought that seeing death as necessary is the first step that we take toward dissolving the necessity.

Death gives us plenty of reminders. We don't even need as reminder the passing of relative or friend, when we see every leaf that falls and every autumn that turns to winter, every dead animal at the roadside and every pet that dies. We see endings even in our own lives, as school sadly turns to job, job sadly turns to another job, and relationships, even dear and intimate ones, come and go. These endings foreshadow our demise. They might not even be painful at all if our own end didn't ferment them into searing finitude. Not only our many interim endings but the beginnings, too, remind us of our ultimate end. Babies, infants, and children are so dear to the elderly precisely because the sight of them focuses the elderly's mind on age and nearing end. New life mocks old life, or if not mocks it, then brings its antiquity into sharp focus. How could I be *so old* in the presence of this tiny newborn life?

Heidegger, in his usual only-partly-fathomable way, helps us in his *Being and Time* to open again the possibilities of death. Our end already *is*, he says, in our being. We do not truly hold death at arm's length, whether death is near or far, or we *should not*. Death is our way, yes, an uncertain way, but a way nonetheless, one that we travel better by embracing it. Death, like other ways, has no specific destination because it is only a way, not a solution or answer. Walking in death's way helps bring death to light, revealing things about it that bring meaning and life to the way. One may walk in darkness through the valley of the shadow of death, or one may walk in light through the same dark valley. Death's contemplation makes the way light rather than dark, when light can show us important markers along the way. Heidegger would have us explore death not as future event but instead as current phenomenon affecting our present being. Because death, more than anything else, constitutes our existence or being, we must live toward death, adopting stances that appropriate death into our identity and being. Death doesn't defeat being but by contradicting being forces being to the meaning that being must constitute. You only truly live by preparing to die. Death demands existential integrity.

Heidegger helpfully discerns death as certain, indeterminate, insuperable, and non-relational. No one entirely escapes death. Death is coming for us all, and so we should all deal with it. Yet we do not know when death will arrive. Death may be instant, or it may be tomorrow, or it may be many tomorrows away. The very young have no guarantee of long life, just as the very old may have many more days than one might expect. Infants die, very sadly. Yet those who are already eighty years old may live for another twenty or even thirty years. One never quite knows. Conditions may make impending demise obvious, but then recovery miraculously ensues. Conditions may conversely be entirely benign, but then *wham*, life is suddenly over. We must thus also somehow deal with death's indeterminacy. Heidegger further regards death as something that one cannot overcome. Physical exercise, healthy diet, quality medical care, and good living at best extend and improve life a little but mean nothing in the face of death. And death is something with which we must each deal alone, when it swiftly or finally comes, Heidegger concluding that no one can take your death away.

Heidegger gathers these phenomena of death into a useful way of thinking about living. Although we experience time as a march toward an end, such that some would recommend that we live as much as possible in the moment, living is never truly in the moment. Being, existing, is instead always a forward-looking exercise, always a making and remaking of the being's soul. We are never quite who we are or what we are because we are instead always becoming someone or something else. We are never finished but instead always unfinished, while striving toward possibilities of who we might ultimately be. Indeed, life is exactly that set of unrealized possibilities, the exhaustion of which means that we no longer live. Because of the constant new possibilities of life, we find the time always too soon to say who we are, until we die, when we find the time too late. Far from a discrete and singular future event, death instead conditions our possibilities now, impelling us to explore them with an urgency that death alone creates. Death's possibility or potentiality of our no longer being able gives meaning to our present ability.

Nietzsche captured uniquely something of this potentiality and its urgency in his conceiving of the *eternal return*. What if a demon bound each of us to live the same life repeatedly into eternity, experiencing again and again all life's pains and regrets while knowing that we would do so and having no capability of changing the pattern and outcome? Wouldn't doing so become utter despair and ultimate madness, unless we were somehow first to have embraced that end? Only if we knew well in advance of death that endless repetition of the same life would be our end would we have any possibility of living life in a way that we sought such end. We should live in such a way as to fervently desire the demon's eternal return, using the demon's own ploy to transcend the demon's trap. Nietzsche's construct reminds us that the only way to defeat a more-powerful enemy is to turn the enemy's greater power against it. Constant imagining of death lies fruitfully upon our actions.

Philosopher and theologian Dallas Willard in *The Divine Conspiracy* addresses directly the kind of inner life that philosophers have from antiquity to today sought to discern, as fruitful in the face of term-limited life. Plato was among the earliest to treat systematically the question of the right condition of one's soul, in a way that the modern secular mind can still appreciate, even though he wrote centuries after the great Jewish prophets had thoroughly covered that ground. Plato focused on the inner attitude or stance that one must take, out of which to live intentionally, to be in the right, good, or just position that life and death together demand. His student Aristotle conceived of that condition more like *virtue*. Whatever the term and specific connotation one prefers, the effort was to connect the inner self with some outward standard. The Jews discerned that outward standard to be the commands of God. Not long after Plato and Aristotle, in antiquity's terms, Christ fulfilled the standard not as a set of commands but as the incarnate God fully reflecting his attributes in human and thus knowable form. Christ's coming and teaching made pursuit of the right standing for life and death a matter not of rule but relationship.

Nietzsche, of course, famously announced, through the madman character in *The Gay Science*, the death of God. As law professor Brian Leiter writes in *The Death of God and The Death of Morality*, in doing so Nietzsche was not simply attacking religious bases for ethical action but also Enlightenment egalitarianism, indeed anything metaphysically rational. The people in the crowd to whom the madman announced God's death were already atheists. Nietzsche was not just rejecting religion but instead *all* moralizing, especially that of the secular metaphysicians and moralists, as his next work *Thus Spoke Zarathustra*, a parody of Christian teaching, elaborated. Nietzsche discerned that when God figuratively dies, so does all morality because moralists no longer have any metaphysical basis for their assumption that society should treat humans as equals. As necessary decisions around dying and death tend empirically to prove, we are not in material terms all equals. Some of us are younger, healthier, smarter, richer, and more influential and resourced than others, while others of us are older, less well, not so wise, poorer, and less well connected than others.

Nietzsche's survival-of-the-fittest, will-to-power approach accepted those empirical and material terms at face value without imposing any moral restraints against their meaning. In Nietzsche's world, death's definition would not depend on one's sentience, or rationalizing, or even on pragmatic abilities and actual needs. All thought, all reason, depends on belief, on faith of the moral, metaphysical, and ultimately religious kind, Nietzsche discerned. Throw away reason, faith, belief, and morality, and one has only Nietzsche's non-rational will to power. Yet in throwing away reason, the ultimate empiricist Nietzsche denies his own empiricism, for what are we if not rational creatures? Nietzsche himself was rationalizing when arguing for rejecting rationality. How we think about and treat death needs its rationale because we do indeed think and rationalize. Thankfully, we do not live in Nietzsche's non-rational, will-to-power world. The world is not entirely natural so long as we are around to examine and shape it according to our will.

In sum, the certain prospect that we die gives some significant degree of meaning to life. The meaning that one draws from death to life can be so strongly negative as death making life meaningless, or moderately negative that death haunts life, or moderately positive that death accentuates and relieves life, or gloriously positive that death concludes life in eternal reward. Whatever one concludes, though, one cannot soundly conclude that death has no meaning for life, unless one adopts a sort of fatalism. Now, there's a loaded word: *fatalism*. Essayist James Baldwin in *The Fire Next Time* referred to the earth turning for the sun inexorably to rise and set until it goes down for the last time for each of us. He further sees everything including religion, politics, culture, violence, and beliefs as denying the fact of death, which he regards as the *only* fact that we possess. Fatalism, though, is a wholly unsatisfactory answer. What we ought instead to draw is neither fatalism nor doctrine but the richest possibility in the face of death's unknown, what the spiritual would call *faith*.

~

Many had anticipated something special in the memorial service, which as it turned out met and exceeded those expectations. The decedent would at birth have been an unlikely nominee to bring together such a large and diverse number of attendees to memorialize and celebrate a life. He had such obvious and significant mental and physical deficits, or perhaps better to call them *anomalies* because they were hardly deficits to him, that by the time that he died well into his twenties he remained in his parents' care at home. Yet his zest for life had combined with his anomalously weak social controls to produce an extraordinarily uniting figure. He had lived large, to be sure, unconstrained by disabling conventions. He was, for instance, a sports fanatic, showing a devotion that others tempered with alternative distractions. But moreover, he had lived utterly without pretense, apparently incapable of the subtle disguise that so critically disarms the rest of us from true relationship. And so, he had friends and supporters who drew more *from* him than contributed *to* him, in both low and high places, friends who, even if they had wished, could not escape his welcome embrace. These were the uniting testimonies that his memorial magically produced, packed with prominent high-school and college athletes and their coaches, a major-sports star and his entourage, and the decedent's loving church community and many disabled friends, all celebrating the remarkable legacy of one who had so little to give but gave all that he had, in devotion to the One who in first giving all, had welcomed him into eternity.

10

Death and Religion

For God so loved the world that he gave his one and only Son, that whoever believes in him shall not perish but have eternal life.

John 3:16.

What too few physicians, sociologists, epidemiologists, philosophers, and other researchers and practitioners around death fail to respect and appreciate is that spiritual commitments are not consolations or, worse, *illusions* drawn from a convenient smorgasbord of faith traditions. They are not self-contained belief systems disconnected from reality, nor merely helpful fellowships like the Veterans of Foreign Wars or Moose Lodge. Spiritual commitments instead identify and declare truths, or attempt to do so, verified with observation and within experience, in their own way as rigorously as any scientific endeavor. And the discovery, pursuit, and embrace of those spiritual truths have consequences to the dying that are just as great as, indeed far greater than, death's material, medical, epidemiological, social, financial, philosophical, and political truths. Those personal consequences reach beyond the material and social to the core of one's identity, what cultural anthropologist Ernest Becker called, in his book *The Denial of Death*, one's *cosmic significance*. As philosopher Soren Kierkegaard put it in his book *The Sickness unto Death*, despair is to not want to be oneself before God, while faith is being oneself *grounded transparently in God*.

Philosopher Alvin Plantinga acknowledges that nothing proves God's existence, which is instead a matter of evidence, just as science relies not on proof but on evidence and the most-reasonable and predictive premises that one draws from it. Plantinga finds a couple dozen such reasons for God, out of which pastor theologian Timothy Keller, in *The Reason for God*, selects these most-familiar ones. First, scientists generally now accept that the universe, including space, time, energy, matter, and all known laws governing those attributes, began from nothing in a single big bang, the source of which was outside of those attributes. While science tells us nothing of the identity of that source, God is such a prime source. Second, the cosmic eruption had precisely the matter and configuration to support us and our observation of the universe's origin, the odds against which are beyond astronomical, thus evidence of God's intention for us. Third, the conditions are just so persistent and orderly, so *regular* rather than chaotic, as to support us and our observations, as God of order and intention would be. Fourth, the order that we observe is beautiful, spectacular, enchanting, just as a God of love and generosity would make it. In awe at the design of creation and our creativity as creatures, we perceive rationality in natural laws, truths in rational principles, and aesthetic in art, music, and literature, with hearts and minds made for God's design.

The secularist says that we project these things onto the universe, but if *everything* is a projection, then so, too, is the secularist's theories, including the projection theory, and including all other science. Anyone who attempts to argue from a foundation of rationality, as secularists more than any of us do, presumes the existence of a source-from-outside who creates and regulates all things, as the universe's foundation. Faith in an orderly, regular, fine-tuning source-from-outside, whom we conventionally name God, is indeed the grounds of science and all other method and theory. One must first have faith in judgment, faith in observation, faith in order, faith in regularity, and faith in design, simply to propound and then test a theory. If instead we had only projection, then we should find no order, regularity, pattern, or design from which to fashion and judge our illusions. Not just our ability to rationalize events and observations against standards, but even our aesthetic judgments of beauty, love, generosity, justice, and dozens of like attributes, including our strong sense of right and wrong with concomitant moral outrage, require trusting in an outside-the-observer and outside-the-observation standard. If we are only higher-level animals surviving in a purely material world by projecting our morals, then we have nothing against which to measure our morals, no powerful sense of God-borne and God-gifted human dignity. We may as well live then as the animals live with a will to power, just as many of us have so chosen to live, never mind God's commands of love, peace, and justice.

That spiritual commitments take so many forms does not mean that all faiths are false and none true, all illusions and none real. Just as physicians and others in the medical arts have been right and wrong, discerning and not discerning, at times and in ages, in their views on the causes and nature of death, so, too, may anyone be headed in right or wrong, helpful or unhelpful, authentic or unreal directions in their spiritual exploration. To be spiritual, whether inside or outside of any religious tradition, does not mean to dive into a pool of relativism, where every spiritual experience gets one equally wet. Faiths can and do share truths. Conversely, faiths, even major worldwide faiths or major sects within faiths, can and do miss exquisite truths that other faiths hold. Our individual pursuit of those spiritual truths, and the eternal consequences that their discovery and embrace entail, is a critically useful, valuable, and wise, indeed necessary pursuit while living and especially while dying. The meaning of life and demand of death lies nowhere else but in those spiritual discoveries. Although I remain an intrepid spiritual explorer, I have discovered and most earnestly embraced those necessary truths, and know what they mean to me and others in life and death. Have you? One yearns to see more of the above brilliant secular experts on the material aspects of death, and their alternately humorous, voyeuristic, and mordant journalists and commentators, be just a little more self-aware of the limitations of their materialistic views and insolence and condescension of their anti-spiritual attitudes. Among them we find brilliant experts who yet also hold profound faith.

Religious traditions have articulated well-thought-out approaches to death, cataloged in comprehensive studies like

Howard Spiro's *Facing Death: Where Culture, Religion, and Medicine Meet*. Summarizing that catalog runs the risk of generalizing about faiths in ways that their many denominations, sects, and cultural expressions belie. Consider first instead how the modern hospice movement draws spirituality into the process of dying. Christian adherent Cicely Saunders founded modern hospice in London in the 1960s to improve how the terminally ill experience dying in an increasingly medicalized setting. Improved pain control and a family or community environment were only the first two of her strategy's three commitments. Engaging the person's spirituality was her key third initiative. Comfort and social support are not sufficient to help the terminally ill countenance death. The experience of dying must also provide and support deep meaning, profound and spiritual meaning, within whatever religious tradition that the person knew or pursued. Researcher Harold Coward and nursing professor Kelli Stajduhar, in their edited book *Religious Understandings of a Good Death in Hospice Palliative Care*, emphasize both Saunders' deep commitment to Christian faith and her equal confidence that hospice should help its patients draw from other faiths or no religious tradition, in approaching and contemplating death.

Saunders, an evangelical Christian social worker, nurse, and physician, conceived of a good death as one that attended to material matters, family and social relationships, *and* spiritual needs. She led and promoted hospice to help patients achieve whatever they could achieve, even while dying, but especially to embrace the experience's spiritual dimensions. To Saunders, *spirituality* in part meant within the traditional spiritual or moral religious beliefs set in faithful practice. But spirituality also includes discerning and pursuing life's meaning toward a universal sense of wholeness, transcendence, and well-being. In dying, persons should be willing and able to prioritize their activities and thinking, and recognize truth, worth, and value, while addressing the deep sense of loss in being increasingly less able to act, while feeling less than worthy of the ultimate truths and values. Saunders saw that dying persons needed more physical pain relief and better symptomatic care but also needed help and permission to draw spiritual focus from impending death. Saunders' hospice movement helps the dying not only with their physical pain but also their *spiritual* journey. Hospice is not a place, like a hospital or nursing home administering palliative care, nor a stage after having lost hope of recovery. Hospice is a philosophy of care integrating support for persons' spiritual and communal lives into an increasingly technological and medical death setting.

Hospice retains its spiritual component today despite hospice's worldwide spread and its institutionalization into the spectrum of care surrounding death. Hospice ministers to Christians, Jews, Muslims, Buddhists, Confucians, Taoists, and Indigenous faith adherents within communities, institutions, forms, and liturgies honoring each of those traditions. Hospice also provides spiritual support to those who profess no faith and follow no religious tradition, whether characterizing themselves as atheists, agnostics, or otherwise. To do so, Saunders and her faith community, with insight from theologian Olive Wyon but moreover the Spirit's gentle leading, had to navigate the difficult question of the religious or other community within which their spiritual pain relief and social support of the dying would take shape. As research fellow Michael Wright and medical sociologist David Clark write in the chapter *Cicely Saunders and the Development of Hospice Palliative Care*, in the book *Religious Understandings of a Good Death*, Saunders concluded that any specific community would unwisely suggest exclusivity rather than inclusion. Hospice leaders and practitioners would simply proceed, seeing where the Spirit took them. Although founded by evangelicals, underpinned by Christian faith, and supporting traditional religion and individualistic spirituality, hospice would not be a religious order or community.

With that conception, hospice quickly spread worldwide, not just among Christian, Jewish, Muslim, Buddhist, Hindu, and other American, European, and Asian believers, but even to reach Aborigines in Australia's distant islands and outback. And not just the spiritual symbols, liturgies, and practices, but even hospice's physical facilities took the forms and shapes of the religious traditions of the dying patients whom hospice served. In communist nations, hospice workers helped dying adherents recover and celebrate the transcendent hope of long- but secretly held Catholic, Orthodox, Buddhist, and other traditional beliefs. Hospice continues to support divergent faith traditions in helping the dying preserve or recover spiritual understanding. Following is how hospice leaders summarize some of those faith traditions for their workers, drawn from the hospice-supported book *Religious Understandings of a Good Death*.

Anantanand Rambachan, in his chapter *Like a Ripe Fruit Separating Effortlessly from Its Vine*, cautions against summarizing Hindu death traditions because of their diversity and detail but suggests, broadly, that they center on attaining liberty in the form of eternal life in God's presence or identity with the infinite. Hindus may orient their lives to attain in death the fulfillment of life. The process of dying should thus emphasize spiritual attainment of peace of mind, turned away from the material and instead fixed on God, but without neglecting physical comfort and pain control that will aid the patient's peaceful exit from the body. Resolving longstanding relationship conflicts while minimizing distraction over material things may further aid the dying adherent's desired serenity. Hospice volunteers may help the dying adherent attain necessary inward focus by creating a sacred space with an icon of the adherent's chosen God-form, sound shields to promote mantra recitations, and other arrangements for sacred rituals. Modesty in dress, purity in thought, special diet, same-sex caregivers, and cleanliness of body aid the dying adherent in treating the body as God's temple. Hindus may hope to die in company of family, whose presence aides should honor and facilitate.

Nursing professor Anne Bruce, in her chapter *Welcoming an Old Friend: Buddhist Perspectives on Good Death*, writes that Buddhism, too, is not monolithic and instead makes room for many ideologies and practices, making difficult their summary, support, and respect. Buddhist death, though, is decidedly a spiritual practice, proving as it does, for everyone including Buddhist adherents, the reality of material impermanence. Compassion through the transition from seeming permanence to proven impermanence thus becomes a key palliative, especially considering Buddhist tendencies to avoid making any tradition or practice essential to the transition. One must respect personal and family beliefs, but the primary attitude may best be one of helping the Buddhist adherent welcome death as an old friend, as simply and peacefully as living by breathing in and then dying by breathing out, with death as opportunity more so than tragedy. The Buddhist conceptions of dying's most-appropriate process may for many rely on truths of suffering, the clinging mind that causes suffering, the antidote of relinquishing the struggle over self and permanence, and the mind's path leading to suffering's elimination. Rebirth beyond death is not new life or second life in like body but instead more akin to transfer of psychic energy or momentum, making the dying adherent's positive, peaceful, and virtuous state of mind at death most critical.

Religions professor Earle Waugh, in his chapter *Muslim Perspectives on a Good Death in Hospice and End-of-Life Care*, likewise questions whether any one approach can adequately support diverse Muslim traditions in dying. Local culture heavily influences the practices of Muslim adherents, as it does for other faiths. Pain as Allah's discipline, though, is a widely accepted conception, to which one should add Islamic-law norms, while recognizing death as an auspicious moment in the believer's life and practice. Respecting institutional protocols for caregivers also supports Muslim adherence. Doctrine indicates that the judged reward of afterlife depends on this life's deeds. Thus, one's eternal destiny has primary significance in this life, giving even greater significance to adherence to Muslim norms in the dying process. Indeed, sickness in general and a last illness especially may constitute winnowing and shaping tests of faith, that the Muslim must bear enduringly without complaint. Last days are a time for reviewing life's relationships, especially those with other Muslims, that death may not come with any ill will toward another adherent. Islamic law may provide for the body's inviolate treatment as Allah's property, discouraging organ harvesting or even autopsy. Daily ritual prayer, seasonal ritual fast, dietary restrictions, and modesty around members of the opposite sex may also affect spiritual support and palliative care.

Professor of Jewish Studies Norman Ravvin, in his chapter *Traditions and Change in Jewish Ideals Regarding a Good Death*, repeats the caution that Jews find widely divergent views within their communities, on end-of-life issues. Orthodox adherents may follow rabbinic interpretations of the law, scriptural paradigms, and

Talmudic narratives on death and dying, while Conservative and Reform communities may accept greater degrees of individual autonomy. Within that variety, one may see prohibitions against hastening death artificially, or reluctance to do so, recognizing the sacredness of all life, but also practical willingness to remove obstacles to swift natural progression of terminal disease. Guiding scriptural narratives highlight simple intimacy, prophetic sense, and attention to duty within family, grounded in self-consciousness to the point of willfulness to the end, eschewing the rituals, tokens, or sacred spaces of other traditions. Early Jewish narratives may say little about what follows death, continuity perhaps instead lying more within lived tradition than transcendence. A later ethos, post-dispersion, projects a messianic kingdom of heaven to which the dead, whose confessions wrote their names in the Book of Life, will rise, while others inscribed in the Book of Death will lie in everlasting shame. The death in her care of a Jewish patient in 1948 inspired Cicely Saunders to found the hospice movement.

Theology professor Janet Soskice, in her chapter *Dying Well in Christianity*, likewise finds diversity in the Christian experience of death. Jesus's life, teachings, mission in death, and life in resurrection guide Christian adherents to found hospitals and hospices, and care for the diseased and dying. Jesus tells his followers to heal the sick and raise the dead, for whatever we do for the sick is to do for him. Sacrificial service to the living and dying, though, is not the means of entering the promised kingdom of heaven but rather evidence that one already follows Christ there, anticipating like resurrection. Thus, death requires no universal ritual but instead shared core faith. Christians ground that faith not on developed doctrine but on the historical record of Jesus's life including the wide, transformative, and costly but gainful witness of his resurrection. Sickness and death, although enemies against which to fight both spiritually and materially, are not punishment or discipline but instead to reveal God's redemptive work, carried out when Christ died willingly to live again in defeat of death. Jesus is not a prophet or messenger but God in flesh. We, like the Christ whom we confess, bear God's image and thus anticipate like resurrection after death, although placing different degrees of emphasis on it. Christians have already died in baptism and live new life in Christ. Confession of Christ as Lord, acknowledgment of such need to have his cleansing sacrifice to approach a holy God, and trust in Christ's historical resurrection are requisites of the faith. God, who creates, also saves, not as reward for a good or disciplined life, for none other than God's Son have sufficient goodness or discipline to approach God, but instead as sign for the coming restoration of all things. Resurrection may be inconceivable to the scientific mind but is not incoherent and certainly not impossible for God who created space and time. Thus, when God demands trust in it, the follower of Christ submits gladly to the welcome demand, made possible by such enormous sacrifice. Hospice thus does not help the Christian die but instead help the adherent to live well while dying, comfortable and assured of God's love. In giving the dying that confident and comforting aid, we are the hands and feet of God.

Modern hospice, though, had more work to do than to address the spiritual needs of terminally ill adherents to the world's major faiths. Christianity had for two millennia underpinned hospice, just as it had birthed the modern hospice movement. Yet an unmooring of spirituality from religious traditions was going on in the West beginning in the 1960s, just as the modern hospice movement spread. Many more in the West were claiming spiritual forms, needs, and interests, outside of traditional religions, leading the modern hospice movement in places to set aside religious support in favor of generalized spiritual coaching. Religion professor Kathleen Garces-Foley, in her chapter *Hospice and the Politics of Spirituality* in the book *Spirituality in Hospice Palliative Care*, cautions that in polarizing religion against spirituality, the hospice movement has run the risk of denigrating religion, making a loser of Christianity especially, while also at times excluding the obvious winner spirituality from the richness of spiritual resources within traditional faiths and their communities.

Garces-Foley argues that a spiritual-but-not-religious revolution has not in fact happened in the United States or even modern hospice's birthplace Britain. Yet the psychological model of personal reflection, life review, and expressed feelings that came to dominate the American hospice movement shunted aside traditional spiritual care, including the chaplain role. The standardization of hospice that new federal funding demanded accelerated the trend, jeopardizing not only hospice support of traditional faiths but also the sensitivity necessary for the new, more-subjective forms of individual spirituality. By universalizing spirituality, the modern movement tended to remove cultural, historical, and local aspects. The movement psychologized spiritual care into conversations about resentment, guilt, anger, and fear, with the objectives of relieving stress and promoting personal growth, while treating Christian patients who insisted on traditional religious observance, as *in denial* and, worse, as *troublemakers*. The movement meanwhile romanticized minority faiths, sparing their adherents the condescension shown to Christians. The movement also coopted and medicalized religious practices, without disclosing their roots, into relaxation techniques, acupressure, aromatherapy, music therapy, and hypnotherapy. Racial minorities especially resisted hospice, some discerned because of its rejection of traditional religious forms and adoption of New Age substitutes.

Religions professor Paul Bramadat and health-sciences professor Joseph Kaufert, in the chapter *Religion, Spirituality, Medical Education, and Hospice Palliative Care* in the same book, track how a similar narrative has influenced medical education and the medical profession to minimize the important role of spirituality and religion in the dying process. Modern trends in the West have loosened individual commitment to specific denominations while raising the prospects for long-term unattached spirituality. Medicine extends that narrative into a secularist ideology, as if history has unfolded away from religions and should continue to do so. Rather than recognizing the widely prevalent religious practices that have long supported science and medicine, and patients in the dying process, religions that birthed and fostered those disciplines and continue to teach and inform them, the narrative dichotomizes the world, pitting the secular and scientific against the religious. Medicine's secularist stance may have spurred research in areas and contributed to vast improvements in public health, but at costs such as ethics scandals, and with backlash spawning alternative medicine and evidence-based approaches. Medicine has responded with humanities curricula, bioethics research, and new interest in the social determinants of health. Yet medicine's pragmatic and secularist hidden curriculum continues to make difficult including serious spiritual and religious attention in the medically managed dying process.

The just-mentioned evidence-based approaches to medicine have indeed found data supporting the positive role of spirituality in the dying process, as palliative-care researcher Shane Sinclair and psychiatrist Harvey Chochinov report in their chapter *Research and Practice: Spiritual Perspectives of a Good Death within Evidence-Based Health Care* in the same book. They conclude that the most compelling evidence, though, is in the reports of the dying themselves, who consistently call spirituality vital at life's end. Indeed, sensitive spiritual care at life's end may be vital even when, or especially when, spirituality remains undefined, as for the atheist, agnostic, or spiritual-but-not-religious patient, concludes literature professor Patrick Grant, in *Tragedy and the Eternal Yea* in the same book, addressing end-of-life questions an atheist might raise in hospice care. No one is quite as others define, just as we are not quite as we try to define ourselves. What we elide from our self-definition when dying may be precisely the portal through which others may reach and touch us as we die, and through which we, when dying, may reach and touch others, in comforting or even transforming ways.

Thus, those many who draw on faith as death nears may face greater spiritual challenges than at any other time in life. Consider that clear thinkers (or those who *try* to be precise and clear because, after all, what clarity can language and thought really claim?) define death as the *irreversible* loss of function in the whole person. Philosophy lecturer Christopher Belshaw gives death that definition and then explains the significance of irreversibility to it. People do momentarily lose heartbeat (cardiac function), stop breathing (pulmonary function), and even cease brain waves before recovering those functions. They may have fallen into water, or suffered severe shock or trauma, only to have rescuers reach and resuscitate them in time for renewed cardiopulmonary function and, with it, brain activity. We don't exactly call those people, in their interim functionless state, *dead*, although we may refer to near-death experiences or even to one being brought back to life. While death's standard cardiopulmonary and brain-activity standards don't on their own account for technological resuscitation, and thus do not account for the irreversibility criterion for death, one hopes that our medical practices do so take account.

Religions may reject the irreversibility criterion, or they may perceive of a different form of new, transformed, or resurrected life. Jesus raised several from the dead including Lazarus and then rose from the dead himself, according to hundreds of eyewitnesses some of whom lost their lives for their insistent testimony. Crowds of thousands followed Jesus's ministry in part because of his miraculous raising of several dead. Those who accept the historical records and accounts, and with them, religious faith, though, are not the only ones facing the irreversibility challenge. Technology has made resuscitation more possible than it once was, extending at least somewhat, even if only briefly, the period where life seems absent but may still arise once again. Cryogenics or other methods extend organ life to the point that technicians can ship organs cross-country for implant. People even hope for the resuscitation of cryogenically preserved relatives, or themselves, long after death. Those who accept historical accounts of resurrection need place no stock whatsoever in such hopes of technological reversibility, but the point remains that concepts of life after death are not restricted to the religious.

Religious adherents also need not rely on near-death experiences to strengthen or confirm their adherence. Some do take encouragement from those near-death accounts, remarkable in content, number, and circumstance, while other adherents reject the accounts or their relevance. Surprisingly, science journalist Teresi reports in *The Undead* that studies of near-death experiences show no correlation between the religious views of the study subject and the number or quality of the reported experiences, except that those having them become more religious or open to spiritual experience. Perhaps spiritual life, whether before or after death, should not be the subject of measurement and instrument, even if it were capable of being so.

Secularists reject religious interpretations of death. Philosophy professor John Messerly writes in *The Meaning of Life* that it "does us no good to imagine that the meaning of life is to know, love, and serve the gods in this life, and to be with them forever in heaven, if there are no gods or heaven," a stance, by the way, on which religious leaders also agree. Messerly presumes, though, no effect to prayer and feels that religious beliefs are wishful thinking, concluding that accounts of Moses and Jesus are fictional, even though the author admits that religious beliefs could solve life's meaning if true. Messerly, though, asserts that religious belief makes personal lives guilt-ridden and misogynistic, and religious nations medieval, authoritarian, and anti-progressive—in other words, makes us and nations worse. No, Messerly concludes at the end of his book, "the abyss, as much as we wish otherwise, always accompanies us," and thus adrift, "we must save ourselves." Happy thought there. Anyone have a lifeline?

Condemnations of religion as the cause for human conflict, neuroses, and primitiveness take inadequate account of modern, never mind ancient, reality. The twentieth century was not the most-violent and deadly century in human history because of religion but instead, arguably, because of its absence. Godless national socialists exterminated six-million religious Jews, while godless communists, imperialists, and fascists killed many more millions of religious and non-religious persons, using irreligious authoritarian regimes. The godless Marx and Nietzsche were their inspiration, not the patriarch Moses or benevolent Jesus. Indeed, the twentieth century may well have martyred more Christians than all twenty prior centuries added together.

Others writing about death treat the religious kindlier, substituting a sort of compassionate condescension for Messerly's brutal condemnation. Cardiologist and medical professor Warraich, in *Modern Death*, writes sympathetically of the religious *clutching* their token symbols, while praying, sometimes successfully he admits in part, for miraculous recovery of their vegetative relative. The religious, he feels, though, are only painting reality, looking through prisms for things that only they see. Religion provides support, not the real. We only imagine a supernatural god, not experience him, because nature makes us prone to finding agency in the purposeless. Or maybe instead, Warraich also writes, still sympathetically, sociologists have the answer that religion serves societies functionally. In any case, without death, Warraich asserts, we would have no religion, a concept that we get implanted in our subconscious at inception. The medical world just needs, he feels, to recognize how much these religious prisms affect their patients, modulating patient fears of both medicine and death. Warraich ends his treatment of death, medicine, and religion with an admiring account of a woman who voluntarily died watching the Food Network, as he saw it, out of her *limitless* strength at having no need for religion. In death, each to his or her own. May your choice, though, be of more consequence than the Food Network.

~

Her aged mother, having already long outlived a fair allotment of anticipated days, was finally near the point of death. Her mother's impending demise worried her because her mother, though a lifelong church attendee, hadn't recently made a clear profession of faith. Her religion had been so comfortably conventional that it had not called on her to rely openly on her Lord. Indeed, her mother had too-often expressed that attaining heaven was a matter of good-enough rather than a matter of relying fully on the Lord's sacrificial grace. Yet then, her mother had gradually struggled awake from what everyone had thought was a dying slumber. A few days later, her mother told her why she had struggled to remain. Her mother had descended a dreaded dark tunnel, only to call on her Lord. The calling had brought her back in full realization of the necessity of his grace. And so, she lived in grace for another year before a blissfully peaceful demise.

11

Death Defeated

I am the Living One; I was dead, and now look, I am alive for ever and ever! And I hold the keys of death and Hades.

Revelation 1:18.

Philosophers, like the French semiotician Jacques Derrida in *The Gift of Death*, say that no one can die in your place but that to die is instead something that you must do for yourself. Yet as nearly everyone worldwide now knows, one extraordinary man professed to do exactly that, dying for us so that we need not die alone for ourselves. Of course, everyone also knows the extraordinary man's offer to be the great divide having to do with death. Do you wish to die alone, as Derrida and so many others encourage that you do, or would you rather accept that this extraordinary man died for you so that you may not die alone but instead live resurrected life? The good news is that you get to choose for yourself. Derrida was thus incorrect in his assertion in an important way. He was *correct* in saying that you may die his way, *alone*, simply by following his instruction to believe what he asserts. Yet he was *incorrect* when he ignored the historical fact that this extraordinary man gave you the choice of dying not alone but in him. Derrida further ignored not just the historical fact of the extraordinary man's offer but also the abundance of philosophical or, if you prefer, metaphysical support for the proposition. Derrida should have said that one *has* died in your place, but you may still die alone if you prefer. The choice is yours: alone, or relieved of a lonely death through his extraordinary intervention and assistance.

In this historical and philosophical context, philosopher and theologian Dallas Willard in *The Divine Conspiracy* properly labels as *subversive* Jesus's life, words, and offer. Christ has been the world's primary historical force for twenty centuries based on just three public years of backroads existence, which should tell the thinking person something about Christ's import. The vain trappings of a royal entry are so, precisely because the matter is less important than it wishes to appear. The opposite was true in Christ's case. His entry's humility would greater reflect its can't-miss-it profundity. Yet many today mistakenly see Jesus as an interesting and maybe even magical figure whom law, meaning the things that we must do, and dogma, the things that we must believe, constrain and define. To believe so is to miss entirely his character and the character of his teaching, both of which have instead to do with disrupting the patterns of law and limits of dogma, to resurrect and restore life. His purpose was that his life, words, and actions would overwhelm and exile deadly law and dogma. His historical entry with disruptive new information and action supplied the extraordinarily free and life-giving answer to millennia of prior philosophical and theological rumination over humankind's dead end.

Christ's offer has little to do with one's trying to live *his way*. Rather, Willard describes the offer as to live *in his presence*. The presence of his Spirit, his supremely powerful nonphysical presence, gradually strips away the pretense of who one wants to be, replacing pretension with the authenticity of who one is. Our spirit, nonphysical but substantial because formed of our valuing, choosing, and thought, is likewise powerful, although not nearly so powerful as his Spirit from which our spirit draws. The Spirit does not diminish us but rather extends the range of our effective will, as Willard articulately describes it. God made us for dominion, to rule. His Spirit perfects in us that capacity to rule, even to the point of extending our rule beyond death into eternity. Yet that rule also exists for us today within God's realm, which is near, indeed as Willard argues, within, around, and accessible to us. Heaven, God's realm, surrounds us, imbuing the world, from which God withdraws only in part, leaving as evidence his realm's spectacular beauty. Christ's invitation is to dwell in that realm, in his presence, now and later, much later, indeed to eternity, always to our greatest benefit, just as to his benefit also, where all that is good God preserves, and all that is not good God destroys.

Tolstoy, for famous example, recovered from years of depression over the seeming futility of his fabulously successful writing career and, moreover, his entire life, when he realized that life in the spirit is not futile precisely because it conquers death. The human condition, Willard argues, has always been a desperate search for something deeper than material existence alone holds. Jesus promises that those who come to depend on him and thus share his life will never die, never even see or taste death. He knew our fundamental problem, and he knew *and provided* its only known solution, whether one accepts that solution or not. And oddly to our modern, materialistic and rationalizing way of thinking, his subversive solution was not information but relationship. People of other cultures and days, including the ancient Jews among whom Jesus taught, would have understood that relationship changes circumstance more so than information. That rule has held true in politics, professions, business, communities, associations, and families but is especially sound when the relationship is with the universe's creator and continuing master.

So, martyrs have held, from the time of the New Testament forward. The Bible's book of Acts records the first martyr Stephen suffering stoning at the hands of the religious leaders after performing wonders while preaching Christ's wisdom. The leaders had stoned Stephen after he professed to seeing the heavens open with Christ standing at God's right hand. As stones knocked him to his knees, Stephen prayed that God would forgive those who killed him, among them the soon-to-be-apostle Paul. History credits Polycarp, serving the church when the disciples who lived with Jesus were dying and a critical second generation of followers arising, for the first recorded post-New Testament martyrdom, burned willingly at the Roman stake after his calm but steadfast rebuke of the examining proconsul. Polycarp shares the earliest-martyrs honor with Ignatius who, like Polycarp, had to argue with friends to let him die, indeed that *fire and cross, flocks of beasts, broken bones, and dismemberment* might be his happy witness to Christ. Perpetua in the third century dying in Roman hands, Thomas Becket in the twelfth century and Thomas Cranmer in the sixteenth century both dying in dispute with England's royal rulers, Joan of Arc in the fifteenth century dying a war heroine still in her teens, and Dietrich Bonhoeffer in the twentieth century executed by the Nazis, are other noted martyrs, among whom history names thousands.

Consider, then, some of the common objections to Christ's extraordinarily generous offer, as to which we each have such a clear choice. A first objection is that Jesus never existed and is instead a myth manufactured and embellished centuries later. To the contrary, his follower Paul wrote thirteen or fourteen of the New Testament's letters (one authorship is uncertain) outlining Christ's extraordinary life while attesting that Christ was God incarnate, within fifteen to twenty-five years of Christ's death. Paul confirmed his own accounts with hundreds of other eyewitnesses. Matthew and John wrote their Gospels from having *traveled with Jesus* as disciples, while Gospel-author Mark was a companion of the disciple Peter and Gospel-author Luke wrote from the testimony of many other eyewitnesses. As ancient documents, experts find Paul's letters and the Gospels highly reliable, far more so on objective measures such as the number and date of the surviving texts, than any other ancient documents the historicity of which goes unquestioned. By contrast, the non-canonical Gnostic gospels arose more than one-hundred years after the original Gospels had established their widespread authority, and thus their accuracy, among people who walked and talked with Jesus, before his death and after his resurrection. The Gnostic gospels work fine as a philosophical system, if you are into Gnosticism, except that first-century Jews held no such beliefs, and the original Gospels were clearly no such contrived system but instead accounts of specific encounters. The original, canonical Gospels are astounding accounts of events that the writers recorded without pretense of making systematic sense of them. They are *reportage*, not in any sense like earlier, contemporary, or later fables, but instead consistent with what experts know of the attributes of collective memory of real events.

Others argue that although Christ existed and may have lived a life and suffered death much as the Gospels record, he simply did not rise from the tomb in which followers placed his dead body under Roman guard. Pastor theologian Timothy Keller, in *The Reason for God*, points out that the earliest resurrection accounts are in Paul's letters, written just fifteen to twenty years after the event, mentioning the hundreds of eyewitnesses. Keller then refers to the analysis of theologian and scholar N.T. Wright who, in *The Resurrection of the Son of God*, supplies the best recent scholarship on the evidence supporting Jesus's resurrection. Wright points out that the Gospels credit the discovery of Jesus's resurrection to the women who returned in grief to the tomb only to discover the body missing. They rushed back to tell the men, while one of the stunned women encountered Jesus there, mistaking him for the gardener. If the accounts were instead tales, then men, not women, would have discovered the missing body, because only men could then testify as credible witnesses. Word spread quickly, as other accounts record, and yet no one, not even the Romans or religious leaders, who together had so much stake in refuting the claim, could produce the dead body.

The accounts that hundreds saw the resurrected Jesus, the disciples touching him, talking with him, and eating with him, also draw credibility from their distinction. Keller, referring to both literary critic C. S. Lewis and the scholarship of N. T. Wright, points out that we today assume, with a disappointing degree of *chronological snobbery*, that observers then were credulous, prone to chase after and believe all manner of tale. Yet to the contrary, research shows that non-Jewish cultures of the region held bodily resurrection to be impossible, indeed undesirable even if it were possible, insofar as the soul sought liberation from the body. Jews, likewise, held resurrection of an individual to be impossible, although some believed in the future resurrection of all things on God's renewal of the whole world. The disciples, who were Jews, would also not have imagined Jesus's individual resurrection possible, as doubting Thomas's denials show, until he, too, saw and touched the risen Christ, and thus would not have grounded the new faith on any such tale, not believing in the possibility themselves and knowing that others would also not believe. The Romans executed many other messianic leaders of the period, not one of whom in death garnered a single report of resurrection.

Jesus's resurrection didn't merely stun its witnesses into reporting, recording, and spreading detailed accounts of the event. The event also exploded across the Mediterranean an entirely new worldview, not in the gradual way that philosophical movements arise, but instantly, distinctly, from the eyewitnesses' reports. Witnesses didn't carry their arguments from town to town, building consensus around an emerging system of thought. They instead breathlessly reported the resurrection and only then tried to make sense of its context and meaning, just in the way that we would if we had seen it ourselves. And they did so against political and religious regimes that would persecute and kill them in droves for doing so. One must take account of this history. And why not accept it as true, when all that it does is make *everything* suddenly matter? With this evidence, indeed given the fact that the extraordinary man's book, assembled across much more than a millennium of experience, is the single most-widely read and published book in all history, one must purposefully turn a blind eye not to believe that Christ existed.

People give common reasons for turning that blind eye, for turning away from such substantial evidence. One objection that some raise is that the extraordinary man and those who have gladly accepted his good-news proposition are being unfair to others, like themselves, who would rather not die once alone but want to avoid doing so in a different way. They feel that the exclusivity of Christ's offer diminishes it. One might feel, though, that because the man gave his *life* for this proposition, that *he*, rather than *we*, should get to choose the terms on which others may accept it. What more could he possibly have done for his hearers than to give his life? But personal feelings aside, in legal terms, he is the offeror, so that for anyone to respond that they want *his* remedy but *their* way constitutes a counteroffer. The law correctly holds that a counteroffer rejects and terminates the offer. So again, you choose whether to accept his enormously merciful and gracious offer, but just don't blame Christ with the assertion that his offer should have been broader, narrower, or different. You have no claim against him in that he won't change the terms of his offer. He chose the offer *and then carried out his side.* Now is too late to ask him to offer something different.

Others say that the exclusivity of Christ's offer not only diminishes the offer but also creates world strife among competing offers, and that everyone would be better without that strife. Keller agrees that commitment to one path excludes other paths and that those taking any path tend to marginalize and oppress those taking other paths. We all wish that it weren't so. Yet the problem is with *us*, not necessarily with the paths, although some paths marginalize and oppress more than others. And on that point, Keller defends the extraordinary man's path by noting that it holds the greatest possible seeds for loving reconciliation, rejecting as it does all judging of others, while inviting instead that one accept the extraordinary man and, in loving others, also draw them to him. Keller notes that the remedies that certain secularists, whether Soviets, Communist Chinese, Khmer Rouge, or Nazis, implement to *eradicate* religion are far worse than the alleged religious disease. The twentieth century's unprecedented slaughter of human life was a *secular*, not religious, spectacle. Secularist condemnations of religion are just as exclusive as competing religious doctrines but, as the slaughter attests, unconstrained by religious morals. Christians, Muslims, Buddhists, and others have also judged, condemned, and slaughtered, even if not nearly to the degree as secularists. One cannot, though, reject *every* belief, whether materialist, secular, spiritual, or religious, simply because people will misconstrue and misuse every belief. One has instead to evaluate what each belief offers, taking each offer on its own terms rather than attaching to each offer the behavior of others who have distorted it.

Another objection is that the miracles for which the extraordinary man gets such widespread credit, including especially that he raised the dead and himself rose from death, are impossible. Pastor theologian Keller agrees that the miracles are inconsistent with what science observes of natural conditions but disagrees that science says that the miracles are impossible. Science says nothing of the sort. Science tests for natural causes without attempting to disprove supernatural causes. Science has no test for supernatural causes because its natural methods bind it to natural observations.

Science cannot, for instance, surmise from observation and then rigorously test for conditions that existed before its big bang, to discover or rule out an immanent, pre-existent intelligence authoring the big bang. While evidence of that being may be everywhere in the being's glorious laws and designs, science could neither prove nor disprove the being, unless of course the being submitted to proof such as by taking on a certain extraordinary man's body. Science, as mathematician philosopher John Lennox says, does not underpin and circumscribe *all* rational thought. Logician philosopher Ludwig Wittgenstein properly held that science describes natural conditions, without explaining their cause or addressing why they should be so, inquiries that we must commit to other rational thought.

Others object that even if science cannot prove or disprove miracles or the supernatural or divine, Christianity as a specific expression of faith conflicts with science, for which they therefore condemn it. Once again, Keller shows in *The Reason for God* that while one can find individual Christians who reject science or aspects of it, such as that humans developed from lower life forms, other Christians see no such conflict, not even with evolution, as to which the world's largest church, the Catholic Church, has published official supportive statements. Indeed, Christianity as an institution has at times been a cradle to science and continues to find adherents among world-class scientists in many fields. Christianity does not conflict with naturalism. Christianity only conflicts with *philosophical* naturalism, which demands that *everything* has a natural and *only* a natural cause, while philosophical naturalism simultaneously demands that the cause is not a cause at all but simply randomness. That kind of exclusive naturalism, represented in Richard Dawkins' *The God Delusion*, is not science but philosophy. Contrast Dawkins' view with that of the eminent research scientist Francis Collins, head of the Human Genome Project, who while embracing evolutionary science simultaneously sees a divine creator in the universe's exquisite fine-tuning, and is a convert from atheism to Christianity, all expressed in his book *The Language of God*.

Indeed, an odd thing about miracles, particularly those that the Bible records, whether a millennium before Christ or through Christ himself, is that embedded within their definition is that they all bear a purpose. Senior fellow and lecturer Eric Metaxas, in his book *Miracles*, points out that miracles are not simply implausible or impossible events, like a horse talking or a monkey writing out a concerto. Instead, miracles point to their author or source beyond the natural. Miracles are specifically *super*natural, designed to draw attention to the creator who makes all things, even the natural, possible. Other inexplicable things that appear to happen but that do not point to the all-powerful and all-good creator God are simply illusion, magic, voodoo, black arts, or whatever you wish to ascribe to them. God does not do miracles for entertainment or to confuse or impress. God does miracles to demonstrate, call attention to, and recruit the senseless and lost to his all-powerful, all-good, supremely loving cause. The Bible's every miracle attests to this same purpose and no other.

Metaxas and other scholars point to Jesus's raising his friend Lazarus from the dead as the supreme miracle example, next to Jesus's own resurrection. After losing his life to a severe illness about which Jesus received ample warning, Lazarus had lain dead and bound in his tomb for four days, a stiff, stinking, and decomposing corpse. Hundreds knew of Lazarus's death, having observed his last illness, confirmed his decease, prepared his dead body, attended its tomb burial, and mourned with his sisters while sending word to Jesus not to bother with his healing because he was *dead*. Jesus's response, that Lazarus died to show God's living miracle to others *so that they may believe*, proves the point of the miracle and all other miracles, calling attention to God as the author of life. In his most extraordinary and revealing statement addressing Lazarus's death, Jesus even said that *I am the resurrection and the life* and that *whoever believes in me will live even when dying* and *will never die*. And, after weeping in humble humanity, Jesus called Lazarus alive. Lazarus rising from the several-days dead and appearing to so many, each of whom now knew that Jesus was the author of life, caused the religious leaders to finally resolve to kill Jesus. As literary critic C. S. Lewis wrote in his book *Mere Christianity*, one must believe Christ a liar, lunatic, or Lord of all.

Thus, the greatest miracle of all, Metaxas asserts, is moving from disbelief to accepting the Lord. Metaxas gives as examples the not just life-changing but also world-changing conversions of atheist Lewis, abolitionist William Wilberforce, and slave trader John Newton, writer of the hymn *Amazing Grace*. Tim Keller, in his *The Reason for God*, describes Christ's entry into the world as God *writing himself into the play*. The God whom even the flies and frogs obeyed when Moses needed another miracle, became a human. Yet God wrote himself into the play not as the all-powerful supreme being that he is but instead as the whisperer toward conversion of souls, offering life beyond death rather than merely demanding due submission. God could have wiped the evil of humankind from the face of the earth, as he did in the time of Noah, starting over. Instead, he gave his own life, dying not just *for* us so that, justice repaid, we could live but also dying *with* us so that he could share in, in fact far exceed, our worst misery. In doing so, God flipped the power script. He proved that materialistic might, armies and gas chambers, survival of humankind's fittest, mean nothing in the face of God's willing weakness. In the greatest act of service ever, God made the oppressed, victors over their oppressors. He freed us even of death.

~

He hadn't been looking for any such thing when it came to him, indeed had never imagined it possible. Yes, his father had long been on his mind. He had prayed for years that his father would come to understand Christ's offer and then reach the point of accepting it. He wanted his father's freedom from death, certainly, but also his father's freedom in current life. He wanted to celebrate his father's victory over death both while his father was here and when his father was hereafter. Yet the victory hadn't come. Then, during a rare period of solitude, prayer, study, and fasting, he had experienced something that had never happened to him before and wouldn't happen since. Suddenly, innocuously, he had felt a hand on his head, a reassuringly gentle hand. He paused, arrested at the sense, as the hand's author had clearly intended. Then, not audibly, and yet not either in that typical narrative with which one thinks through one's day, and instead deep within his soul, he heard a voice that he understood, he knew not how but nonetheless knew, was that of his father's father. *Take care of my son*, the voice said, repeating, *pray for my son, your father*. And the hand gently withdrew. He had only known his grandfather, who had died when he was an infant, from a very few old photographs and a newspaper-clipping obituary. That obituary, though, had become his beacon, revealing as it did that his father's father had known the great Lord, too. His prayers for his father would thus echo prayers that his father's father must have prayed so many decades before.

12

Resurrected Life

I know that my Redeemer lives and that in the end he will stand upon the earth. And after my skin has been destroyed, yet in my flesh I will see God; I myself will see him with my own eyes—I, and not another. How my heart yearns within me!

Job 19:25-27.

Cultures worldwide and throughout the ages have anticipated life after death. Aborigines and Scandinavians have projected heaven as on a far-away island, Central and South Americans on the sun or moon, and Greeks in the Elysian fields, while Native Americans anticipated an afterlife hunting buffalo spirits. Modern Americans, too, believe overwhelmingly in life in heaven after death. Yet do you even want to live eternally? Some say that whether such an option to annihilating death exists or not, they cannot imagine anything good of eternal life. They instead believe that life in eternity must, in its presumably repetitive and boring nature, be quite like hell, as Mark Twain parodied in *The Adventures of Huck Finn*. What, though, if eternal life were instead worthwhile, more so than we can hardly imagine?

Consider the possibility, indeed the benefit, of using your best imagination to anticipate your best heaven. If afterlife exists, then perhaps we have imagination for exactly that purpose, to live now anticipating the richest possible reward for having lived for heaven, not that one earns one's way into heaven, Christ having already done all the earning. Injunctions to *fix our minds on things above* direct us to do exactly that, to think productively about heaven, which inevitably means spending less time thinking about what goes on here. We should, in a sense, let heaven-thinking fuel not just our imagination of futures but also our present lives, as we draw joy from the future if not so much from the present. We permit ourselves to draw small measures of energy and inspiration from the coming vacation, weekend, night out, or cup of coffee. Why not draw vast reservoirs of energy and inspiration from something far more consequential than such small pleasures, like *eternal heaven*? The kingdom of heaven is near. We can draw now from the treasure that we place for the future there.

One of the obstacles to such productive thinking about death, that it means the richest possible reward and that we should thus draw encouragement from it, may be that too few of us feel assured of reaching heaven. We sense that its path is narrow, while broad is the road to destruction. Nothing impure enters heaven, and yet we know how impure we are. I in my present broken state would undoubtedly sully heaven. I must instead take on another's life, the only life worthy of entering heaven, so that I instead enter the only way that I am able, incognito. I must be in the guest book in his name, the name that he has given me, rather than my own name. And I accomplish that substitution, his life for my life, only by accepting his offer to so act on my behalf. He made that offer. To accept the offer, I need only recognize its value, the benefit of the bargain, which is to recognize my need of his substitution to reach the unfathomable, but at least in-part imaginable, reward of heaven. I need only know that my only way in is through him, then to say so, and thereby to accept his offer. Assurance is possible, but assurance only follows this path.

The possibility also exists that heaven is not a single fixed place. Heaven may include a present intermediate realm or state with a future new heaven and earth. Scientists, cosmologists, and philosophers debate the existence and scientific testability of parallel universes, parallel worlds, parallel dimensions, alternate universes, or other such multiverse theories. Some theoretical physicists like Stephen Hawking and Neil deGrasse Tyson favor the theories while others disfavor them, which is not to suggest that the theories bear any relationship to concepts of the afterlife and heaven, only that theories of other current, unobservable worlds are not unique to religion. Proponents of both the theoretical-physics and religious views see those parallel realms, though, as physical and real, perhaps in some instances more real than the world in which we live. For example, some theoretical physicists postulate parallel worlds having several more of our world's limited number of dimensions. Scriptural accounts have heaven's inhabitants in real bodies, with real voices, real memories of their time on earth, and some ability to view current matters on earth. The accounts also give those in heaven some ability to pray for justice on earth. Moreover, scriptural accounts occasionally give an inhabitant on earth a glimpse into heaven. Accounts also assure heaven's future inhabitants that they will join its other inhabitants whom they once knew on earth.

Some religions, for example Buddhism and Hinduism, tend to represent afterlife as intangible rather than physical and largely unknowable rather than definable to any degree. Scriptural accounts in Christianity instead identify heaven as an authentic paradise, indeed a *new earth*, one redeemed from its current corrupted state. If heaven will be a new earth, then we might expect to recognize many of its features as earth-like, including, as scripture mentions, mountains, fruit-bearing trees, animals, and cities filled with houses, in turn filled with people in transformed bodies. We need not anticipate some vague intangible state but should anticipate a familiar landscape with the physical capability to enjoy it. Yet if this landscape is a perfectly redeemed one, then heaven will only be the *best* of earth, *paradise* on earth. Then, too, our physical capability, in resurrected and healed bodies, will be fully up to exploring and enjoying that paradise, even organized as redeemed people, cultures, and nations. If we find life on earth worthwhile, then life in a heavenly new and redeemed earth must be so much more worthwhile, paradise's blessings extended through the whole of the old earth, relieving its every curse.

Scriptural accounts indeed suggest the resurrection of the old earth into a glorious new earth. Our death and resurrection do not divorce us forever from our old home but instead prepare us to enjoy our old home in its equal resurrection. Resurrection of the earth implies at least some aspect of physical continuity. Scripture does not have the resurrected float on clouds but instead occupy a resurrected earth. Why, then, wouldn't our future place have similarly stimulating contours and exciting opportunities? Life after death in a resurrected earth would thus not be a boring affair at all but instead at least as engaging as our present circumstance, and likely far more so, while relieved of all curse. Resurrection of the body also implies physical continuity, bodies healed and transformed to be sure, but *our* bodies in some aspect nonetheless. Thus, scripture does not have the resurrected floating as formless spirits but instead walking, talking cooking, eating, and doing other things that one might wish to do, especially in imperishable body. If life can be good in perishable state, then why wouldn't life doing similar things but in imperishable state be better? That all in resurrected bodies would happily comply in unity with the wholly beneficent desires of an all-loving God would only make the experience far better, especially when God's desire is not merely to rule but instead to love and serve.

In these accounts, heaven may then be a familiar entity, indeed a *home*, rather than a non-entity. Whatever we enjoy of this present entity, we should enjoy even more the new entity, especially if the new entity banishes the pain of the present one. The new entity should have time and space, in dynamic rather than static form. Meaningful activity, in adoration and devotion, and purposeful work and fulfilling relationship, should be ours, as we explore, learn, and discover familiar but fascinatingly renewed landscape, wonders satisfying our every desire. The best part, though, would be encountering heaven's prime resident, whose presence radiates in enlivening light throughout the place. The stadium isn't special when empty but only when the heroes play. Everything that we enjoy of a place, whether here or there, involves those who reside there. A home isn't so because of its special view or comforts. Home is where the family is, where the face of the one who knows and loves you shines toward you, giving you peace. The gifts of heaven aren't because the Father is too busily self-involved, withdrawn, and away. Heaven is a gift because the Father resides there, waiting for you to come home. We have a hard time here seeing the Father in the gifts that he nonetheless supplies us. Accounts of heaven promise that we will see the Father there in every gift.

Those who mistakenly read automaticity, even tedium, into scriptural accounts of continual worship of the Father in heaven miss the meaning. We define worship as authentic, passionate, whole-body and whole-mind devotion to its subject. Picture where you see such genuine worship here, whether at revivals, rock concerts, sports arenas, or elsewhere, and then magnify that picture a hundredfold for how heaven must worship the author of life. Wherever your temptation or addiction lies here, the hole of God's love that we try hopelessly to fill with other than him, imagine your liberty to pursue complete satisfaction wholeheartedly there, not to your detriment but to his glory. Good things that must end here will not end there. Worship should be anything but boring. That worship in heaven is corporate, unified, and orderly, does not mean that we lose our individuality. We find our life and identity in Christ when we lose it to ourselves, when we stop trying to hold onto it to make it our own, which it never was. God does not subsume us in heavenly worship but makes us who we are.

The resurrected life that heaven's accounts urge us to pursue also affects us here. While heaven's gate opens for every child of the Lamb, scriptural accounts hold that we weave here the dress that we will wear there. We gain no access to heaven through our good works here, but our good works here become our reward and raiment there. The management that we exercise here in all corruption will become the management that we exercise there in all dominion. The one city we rule well here will become ten there. The miserly kindness that we show here will be bushels of kindnesses that we show there, the tiny badge here, a crown there. The little things that we relinquish to heaven now will have grown to big things to enjoy and share there. We should find it so because God made all things to reflect his fullness, his super-abundance of good. The good that we do, he invited and arranged out of his fullness, which corruption will not bind in heaven as corruption limits it here. Heaven's reward will be more good works, not fewer, greater responsibility and engagement, not less. And in all activity, every resident will also find rest, satisfying rest.

God's purpose, philosopher and theologian Willard writes in *The Divine Conspiracy*, is no less than to bring a redeemed and resurrected community of persons out of the material and finite into the spiritual and infinite, in somewhat the way described above. God must do so because of his nature as wholly complete and fully effective love, a love that needs others to know. Our ability to examine our existence, question our finite nature, and fear our death fulfills God's need for others who are conscious as he is conscious, to turn to him and know him for the love who he is. Although as the creator he is over all and greater than any, he will nonetheless share his governance of his spectacular creation with those who so choose to know him as love. Here, then, is the mystery of life and its wholly good author, so gently exposed in the life, death, and resurrection of Jesus Christ. Every meaning that we pursue has this answer and end. Whether we are like Plato, Socrates, or Aristotle, or Tolstoy or Nabokov, we intuitively know that we must connect our lives with the immaterial arc of all history. Yet we must learn that in Christ is how we do so.

~

She could laugh about it later, after she had received the confirmation that she sought. She had been close to her father for all her adult life. The two had been friends in the way that fathers and daughters sometimes can be, finding nothing about which to disagree and just taking comfort in knowing and loving one another, laughing together and remembering old times. He had lived a long and full life but one that always had time for her, once she was an adult and able to share in adult things. When he died, she had grieved his loss as any daughter and friend would do. She knew that she should trust that his faith in the great Lord had carried him to the kingdom. Yet she wanted the Lord's reassurance, a sign that her father was in heaven. And so, she had delighted when she had walked by his gravesite late one night, seeing a beautiful oval glow around the headstone, as if illuminated by a shaft of gorgeous moonlight. She returned to the gravesite in wonder the next morning, only to see that the workers who had carved her father's headstone at the site had left a perfect oval of white marble dust that the moon the night before must have illuminated. The Lord hadn't sent a sign after all, or maybe he had, using the worker's dust. Always a gracious Lord, though, he promptly sent her another welcome sign that he held her father in loving embrace.

Conclusion

And I saw the dead, great and small, standing before the throne, and books were opened. Another book was opened, which is the book of life. The dead were judged according to what they had done as recorded in the books.

Revelation 20:12.

Death, the above discussion should clearly support, is a far more complex subject than we tend to grant it, while also far more prevalent in our culture and influential in our thinking. *Get me right*, the subject of death demands, *or you will in living have missed something essential.* Although intensely and ultimately individual, death does not allow us to experience it, learn from its experience, and relate to others our conclusions. Death is thus a subject to which we can relate only through the loss of others, making death somehow essentially social rather than individual. Although final and terminal, and therefore an event that we might prefer to put off and ignore, even until it occurs, death does not allow us to predict and control it. Death thus must inform and imbue our lives lest we fail to draw from it that which living fully and completely demands. And because death is organic and material, death demands that we decide whether we are something more than material organisms and what that decision may mean for our legacy and future beyond death.

Socrates spoke vigorously in defense of charges, for which he would die, that he falsely claimed to be wiser than others while instead by sophistry teaching the Athens young things that were untrue. After due investigation, Socrates indeed admitted that he appeared to be wiser than those who claimed wisdom but who clearly were not wise when he examined them. Yet Socrates measured his own wisdom not by what he *knew* but instead by how he, in contrast to the supposedly wise, knew what he *did not know*. To claim wisdom on subjects that one does not know is to prove that one is unwise. Human wisdom, Socrates concluded, *is worth little or nothing*. So is death, a subject that one cannot fully know. Death's unknowability creates a portal, yes for foolishness as much of the above discussion shows, but also for cautious discernment by the wise. In the vast record of billions of human deaths, and human attitudes toward living and dying, one certainly must see clear clues.

Indeed, Socrates gave some of those clues in professing that he, a wiser person, would not suffer for being killed by the less wise. Instead, he maintained, the less wise survivors would suffer for having killed one sent to them, Socrates said, by the divine. Socrates had from childhood listened to the divine's interrupting voice, he explained to his executioners. That divine voice had often diverted him from what he was about to do or say but had never directed him toward anything different other than to speak truth. Socrates cared not at all about death but cared everything about the just and holy, he explained. He admitted that he did not know whether death was good or bad but *did* know that to do or say anything against the divine and lacking in virtue was to do a very bad thing. And so, when wrongly convicted of the charge, he refused his silence in exile and instead accepted the capital penalty. Socrates saw that one can at least for a time escape death but that to escape wickedness was much harder. He saw that death presented only two choices, one to sleep peacefully unaware forever or the other to face the divine in true judgment. For the virtuous, evil holds no power in living or dying, while the corrupt pay in living and may further do so in dying.

The above chapters on science, medicine, music, art, culture, history, law, philosophy, and religion suggest that in every field and form, we struggle to face death. Science in its ideological form alternately tries to explain us away as if we were only temporary repositories for selfish genes or to crypto-preserve us as if we could live forever as material beings. Medicine alternately tries to keep us alive forever or to let us die or even to kill us and harvest our organs, for the same material reasons. Music in its ideology alternately rages that we are nothing or hints that we could be part of everything, eternal. Art does likewise, on one hand mocking the transcendent while on the other hand pointing to and celebrating it. Culture carries on its own struggle with the metaphysical, alternately distracting us from the deep questions while also turning the profound into ritual. History alternately depicts either an arc, whether despotic or triumphant, or a circle repeating itself endlessly. Law tries to corral death, never quite successfully. Philosophy muses on questions of death that demand so much more than musings. Religion turns the question of death into one of faith in something transcendent, although religions differ on just what transcends.

Death thus imbues fields and forms just as it imbues the life of any individual. Death, the cardiologist and medical professor Warraich writes in his book *Modern Death*, is a primitive experience, as ancient as life itself. Yet he also discerns, as many of the other authors cited above see, that death's ethos has changed as modern society and technologies have changed, blurring the line between life and death. We now know more about why we die, from the microscopic cellular level to the whole-system level, but somehow seem to know less than ever as to when we die or even whether we *are* dead. The new tension of this unwelcome but unavoidable modern dynamic has thrown longstanding rituals, practices, commitments, and meanings into question, loosening social, philosophical, and religious foundations. Now thus seems an important time to examine the answers, attitudes, and approaches as to what we should *do*, individually, to prepare for, countenance, and somehow integrate and address death.

The difference in approaches to death, scientists, physicians, musicians, artists, philosophers, lawyers, and theologians seem in their debates to agree, lies somewhere in *doing* or between *doing* and *done*. Many persons think that *doing* may get one past death into something better, whether that something is heaven, nirvana, bliss, or some other state, or even an unknown deity's embrace. The *doing*, though, is different for the scientist, physician, philosopher, or religionist, indeed different for practitioners within each field. Scientists and physicians may either pursue how to preserve one's telomeres as a prescription against death or conversely tell us that we have nothing at all to do because when the subject is death, we are all done. Musicians and artists may invite participation in life as all that we have or instead as harbinger of all that we may become. Philosophers and theologians offer their own philosophical and spiritual stances, whether in despairing nihilism or hopeful prayer. Let's get on with it, all fields may say, one way or the other, whether in wailing, hope, or rage.

The Christian's millennia-long and quite-unique witness is instead that doing does little to advance one's standing with death because instead the critical work was long ago done. In that death-be-defeated stance, the follower need recover nothing from modern technological advances because the modern and ancient face death alike. Death rituals were also never the answer. Science, medicine, art, music, literature, philosophy, and culture can all say what they wish about death without in the least changing history's course or the universe's makeup. The distinct thing about death is that each of us faces it apart from the constructs through which society, culture, and philosophy invite us to do so. We each make the choice of how to countenance death. If you haven't already done so, then try seeing in death the loving face of the extraordinary man-God who defeated it for you. Face death accepting his offer that you may defeat death, too.

~

He sat bedside, staring at his struggling father, with the nurse sitting on the other bedside. A month had passed since his father's fateful letter firmly and finally rejecting the salvation that the son knew. The father had struggled mightily since then, thrashing and moaning incoherently in bed, even as the doctors and nurses found no cause other than impending demise. The son suspected a spiritual struggle, as angels contended with devils for his father's gathering soul, although who, this side of heaven, was to tell? As they sat bedside, the nurse called the father's name loudly, trying to wake him for some last sustenance, but the father simply continued to moan and toss, eyes closed. The nurse and son took turns patting the father's head and taking the father's hands, trying to calm and console him. Then, it happened. The father opened his eyes wide for the first time in weeks, slapped his forehead in astonishment, and cried, "Jesus! My God, my God, my God!" The father closed his eyes again, now laying still. The son looked at the nurse as if to ask whether she realized the exclamation's spiritual significance. The nurse instead said simply, "He's quiet now," in wonder. And then, shortly later, in peace, his father had embarked on the short trip to heaven.

Epilogue

There is no difference between Jew and Gentile, for all have sinned and fall short of the glory of God, and all are justified freely by his grace through the redemption that came by Christ Jesus.

Romans 3:24.

The subject of death does arrest one, making one take a deeper look at one's life. My own deeper look shouldn't bore you but still might show you what such a look could mean. My middle name is *Pierce*, not spelled *pearce* as is more-commonly the case but rather *pierce*, as to penetrate or impale. Names have meaning. You might know the import of your own name, in which I hope you find deep, special, and essential meaning. My name seems to have meaning that my parents little knew when they bestowed it. *Nelson* is an unusual first name, yes, the first name of a New York governor and a South African civil-rights leader, but more commonly a surname like that of a famous admiral. Take the name apart, though, *ne-el-son*, and it bears more meaning. To be *né* anything is to have had an original name, as in Sarah *né* Sarai or Abraham *né* Abram. *El* in Hebrew means God, as in El Shaddai, meaning God almighty, God of heaven, or God who suffices in glory. And *son* means issue, progeny, offspring. My parents named me a son of God, just as we are all such children. Yet my parents named me not after just any God but the God whom men *pierced*, the God who willingly died hung from a cross to love us to eternity in defeat of death. My parents had little choice in giving me their last name *Miller*, a name that nonetheless bears equal personal meaning to my given names. A miller grinds grain into flour for bread to feed the hungry. The biblical sense of grain is the Word of God, feeding the hungry. True to my name, I grind grain, working with words in happy and diligent effort to share faith, letting the Word of God lift the weight of death from burdened shoulders, replacing it with the light weight of glory. Eat heartily from the grain of life. Eat of his body, and drink of his blood, as he wished so fervently for you to do that he gave you his very life. And in doing so, discover the meaning of your true name. Discover who you are through *his* death, giving you eternal life, rather than *your own* death, unnecessarily alone.

~

He thought of his father's passing frequently over the next few months until the date of his parent's anniversary. Yet he tried not to examine his father's death-bed confession too much. He shared the story with few, wanting instead to preserve it as the great personal gift that it was. He also did not ask God to confirm it, wanting instead to trust God for exactly what he had given his father and given him. His parents' anniversary day passed with only a couple of gentle reminders that both his mother and father were now dead. He hadn't passed the day looking for a sign that both were in heaven, again because he trusted that God had answered many prayers. That evening, he fell asleep only to awake early in the night, gasping for air from the shock of what he at first thought had been a nightmare. He reached instinctively for his smartphone to check for email as he rose and walked down the hall to clear his head of the supposed nightmare, one that now he strangely couldn't quite recall. His smartphone said 11:59 p.m., one minute before midnight, still on his parents' anniversary. The smartphone screen opened to the Bible verse that he must have been reading just before he fell asleep, that those who died in Christ would live again.

At that moment, his dream came back to him. In his dream, his smartphone had rung on the nightstand next to the bed. Still dreaming, he had picked up the smartphone to say *hello*. His father's voice had replied, calling his name in an endearing short form that only his father had used. Still dreaming, the son had gasped for air at wonder and excitement over hearing his deceased father's voice. The son had said *dad, dad,* repeatedly in his dream, as his father continued to call his name. Finally, the son, still dreaming, had asked his father, *where are you?!* His father had chuckled, amused, saying only, *well, now I don't know*, teasing the son when the father clearly did know. Frantic now, though still dreaming, the son had shouted into the smartphone the only thing that he could think to say, which was, *well what's it like there?!* to which the father had replied with another chuckle, *it is good*, drawing out the *good* as if the father was indeed luxuriating in paradise. And the son awoke at the last second before midnight, gasping for air, about to reach for his smartphone on which the message of salvation awaited.

Bibliography
(110)

Alcorn, Randy, Heaven (Tyndale House Publishers 2004);

Anttila-Hughes, Jesse Keith, & Solomon Hsiang, Destruction, Disinvestment, and Death: Economic and Human Losses Following Environmental Disaster (SSRN February 18, 2013);

Aries, Philippe, The Hour of Our Death (Vintage Books 1982);

Aries, Philippe, The Hour of Our Death: The Classic History of Western Attitudes Toward Death over the Last One Thousand Years (Vintage Books 2008);

Barry, Barbara, Lebewohl: Reconstructions of Death and Leave-Taking in Music (Pendragon Press 2013);

Becker, Ernest, The Denial of Death (Free Press 1973);

Bedau, Mark A., & Carol E. Cleland, The Nature of Life (Cambridge University Press 2010);

Bedau, Mark A., The Nature of Life, in Steven Luper, ed., The Cambridge Companion to Life and Death (Cambridge University Press 2014)

Belshaw, Christopher, Annihilation: The Sense and Significance of Death (McGill-Queen's University Press 2009);

Berenguer, Elizabeth Esther, The Invisible Man: How the Sex Offender Registry Results in Social Death, 2 Journal of Law & Social Deviance 92 (2011);

Berry, William W., III, Ending the Death Lottery, 76 Ohio State Law Journal 1 (2015);

Blanco, Maria-Jose, & Ricarda Vidal, eds., The Power of Death: Contemporary Reflections on Death in Western Society (Berghahn 2014);

Bramadat, Paul, Harold Coward, & Kelli I. Stajduhar, Spirituality in Hospice and Palliative Care (SUNY Press 2013);

Bramadat, Paul, & Joseph Kaufert, Religion, Spirituality, Medical Education, and Hospice Palliative Care, in Paul Bramadat, Harold Coward, & Kelli I. Stajduhar, Spirituality in Hospice and Palliative Care (SUNY Press 2013);

Brombert, Victor, Musings on Mortality: From Tolstoy to Primo Levi (University of Chicago Press 2013);

Brooks-Gordon, Belinda, Fatemeh Ebtehaj, Jonathan Herring, & Martin J. Johnson, eds., Death Rites and Rights (Hart Publishing 2007);

Bruce, Anne, Welcoming an Old Friend: Buddhist Perspectives on Good Death, in Harold Coward & Kelli I. Stajduhar, eds., Religious Understandings of a Good Death in Palliative Care (SUNY Press 2012);

Bruhn, Siglind, Frank Martin's Musical Reflections on Death (Pendragon Press 2011);

Capers, I. Bennett, On Andy Warhol's Electric Chair, 94 California Law Review 243 (January 2006);

Casarett, David, Shocked: Adventures in Bringing Back the Recently Dead (Current 2014);

Chau, P-L, & Jonathan Herring, The Meaning of Death, in Brooks-Gordon, Belinda, Fatemeh Ebtehaj, Jonathan Herring, & Martin J. Johnson, eds., Death Rites and Rights (Hart Publishing 2007)

Chin, Gabriel J., The New Civil Death: Rethinking Punishment in the Era of Mass Incarceration, 160 University of Pennsylvania Law Review 1789 (2012);

Chodorow, Adam, Death and Taxes and Zombies, 98 Iowa Law Review 1207 (2013);

Clough, Patricia Tincineto, & Craig Willse, eds., Beyond Biopolitics: Essays on the Governance of Life and Death (Duke University Press 2011);

Collins, Francis S., The Language of God: A Scientist Presents Evidence for Belief (Free Press 2007);

Coward, Harold, & Kelli I. Stajduhar, eds., Religious Understandings of a Good Death in Palliative Care (SUNY Press 2012);

Cusack, Carmen M., Death Revolution: Eating the Dead to Save Our World, 4 Journal of Environmental & Animal Law 37 (2012);

Richard Dawkins, The God Delusion (Mariner Books 2008);

DeGrazia, David, The Nature of Human Death, in Steven Luper, ed., The Cambridge Companion to Life and Death (Cambridge University Press 2014);

Denno, Deborah, The Lethal Injection Quandary: How Medicine Has Dismantled the Death Penalty, 76 Fordham Law Review 49 (2007);

Derrida, Jacques, The Gift of Death, trans. D. Wills (University of Chicago Press 1995);

Dezhbakhsh, Hashem, Paul Rubin, & Joanna Shepherd, Does Capital Punishment Have a Deterrent Effect? New Evidence from Post-Moratorium Panel Data (SSRN October 2003);

Didion, Joan, The Year of Magical Thinking (Vintage 2007);

Earle, Sarah, Caroline Bartholomew, & Carol Komaromy, Making Sense of Death, Dying and Bereavement (SAGE Publications Ltd. 2009);

Fairfield, Paul, Death: A Philosophical Inquiry (Routledge 2015);

Fischer, John Martin, Mortal Harm, in Steven Fischer, ed., The Cambridge Companion to Life and Death (Cambridge University Press 2014);

Fischer, John Martin, ed., The Metaphysics of Death (Stanford University Press 1993);

Foley, Elizabeth Price, The Law of Life and Death (Harvard University Press 2011);

Freud, Sigmund, The Letters of Sigmund Freud (Basic Books 1960);

Garces-Foley, Kathleen, Hospice and the Politics of Spirituality, in Paul Bramadat, Harold Coward, & Kelli I. Stajduhar, Spirituality in Hospice and Palliative Care (SUNY Press 2013);

Gawande, Atul, Being Mortal: Medicine and What Matters in the End (Henry Holt & Co. 2014);

Goswami, Amit, Physics of the Soul: The Quantum Book of Living, Dying, Reincarnation, and Immortality (2d ed. Hampton Roads 2013);

Guerra-Pujol, F. Enrique, & Orlando I. Martinez-Garcia, Clones and the Coase Theorem, 2 Journal of Law & Social Deviance 43 (2011);

Halman, Talat, Death Is Its Own Conquest, in Christina Staudt & Marcelline Block, eds., Unequal Before Death (Cambridge Scholars Publishing 2012);

Hawley, Katherine, How Things Persist (Clarendon Press 2002);

Hawley, Katherine, Persistence and Time, in Steven Luper, ed., The Cambridge Companion to Life and Death (Cambridge University Press 2014);

Horne, John, Screening the Dying Individual: Film, Mortality and the Ethics of Spectatorship, in Maria-Jose Blanco & Ricarda Vidal, eds., The Power of Death: Contemporary Reflections on Death in Western Society (Berghann 2014);

Hujar, Peter, Portraits in Life and Death (Da Capo Press 1976);

Joralemon, Donald, Mortal Dilemmas: The Troubled Landscape of Death in America (Left Coast Press 2016);

Keller, Simon, Posthumous Harm, in Steven Luper, ed., The Cambridge Companion to Life and Death (Cambridge University Press 2014);

Keller, Timothy, The Reason for God: Belief in the Age of Skepticism (Riverhead 2008);

Kohli, Sachin, Pricing Death: Analyzing the Secondary Market for Life Insurance Policies and Its Regulatory Environment, 54 Buffalo Law Review 101 (April 22, 2006);

Kumari, Areti Krishna, Violence from Cradle to Grave (SSRN; March 12, 2007);

LaFrance, Arthur B., Physician Assisted Death: From Rhetoric to Reality in Oregon, 8 Wyoming Law Review 333 (2008);

Lain, Corinna, Deciding Death (SSRN; April 3, 2007);

Lavi, Shai, The Problem of Pain and the Right to Die, in Austin Sarat, ed., Pain, Death and the Law (University of Michigan Press 2001);

Leiter, Brian, Nietzsche on Morality (Routledge 2d ed. 2015);

Leiter, Brian, The Death of God and the Death of Morality, forthcoming in The Monist (August 29, 2016);

Leiter, Brian, The Truth Is Terrible, in Daniel Came, ed., Nietzsche on Morality and the Affirmation of Life (forthcoming Oxford University Press, SSRN February 24, 2014);

Lewis, C. S., A Grief Observed (HarperOne 2001, originally published 1961);

Lewis, C. S., Mere Christianity (Harper San Francisco 2009, originally published 1952);

Luper, Steven, Life's Meaning, in Steven Luper, ed., The Cambridge Companion to Life and Death (Cambridge University Press 2014);

Luper, Steven, ed., The Cambridge Companion to Life and Death (Cambridge University Press 2014);

MacLean, Norman, Young Men and Fire (University of Chicago Press 1992);

Messerly, John G., The Meaning of Life: Religious, Philosophical, Transhumanist, and Scientific Perspectives (Durant & Russell Pubs. 2012);

Metaxas, Eric, Miracles: What They Are, Why They Happen, and How They Can Change Your Life (Penguin Random House 2014);

Miller, Daniel, & Fiona Parrott, Death, Ritual, and Material Culture, in Belinda Brooks-Gordon, Fatemeh Ebtehaj, Jonathan Herring, & Martin J. Johnson, eds., Death Rites and Rights (Hart Publishing 2007);

Nietzsche, Friedrich, Beyond Good and Evil (CreateSpace 2016) (first published 1886);

Nietzsche, Friedrich, The Gay Science (Vintage 1974) (first published 1882);

Nietzsche, Friedrich, Thus Spoke Zarathustra (CreateSpace 2016) (first published 1883);

Nuland, Sherwin, How We Die: Reflections on Life's Final Chapter (Vintage Books 1995);

Oates, Joyce Carol, A Widow's Story: A Memoir (Ecco 2012);

Olson, Eric, What Are We? in Steven Luper, ed., The Cambridge Companion to Life and Death (Cambridge University Press 2014);

Palladino, Paolo, Biopolitics and the Philosophy of Death (Bloomsbury Academic 2016);

Partridge, Christopher, Mortality and Music: Popular Music and the Awareness of Death (Bloomsbury Academic 2015);

Piven, Jerry, Ontological Dread, in Christina Staudt & Marcelline Block, eds., Unequal Before Death (Cambridge Scholars Publishing 2012);

Plato, Crito (Cathal Woods & Ryan Pack, trans., 2016);

Pyszczynski, Tom, Matt Moyl, & Abdolhossein Abdollahi, Righteous Violence: Killing for God, Country, Freedom, and Justice, 1 Behavioral Sciences of Terrorism & Aggression 12 (2009);

Pyszczynski, Tom, & Pelin Kesebir, Culture, Ideology, Morality, and Religion: Death Changes Everything, in M. Mikulincer & R. Shaver, eds., The Social Psychology of Meaning, Mortality, and Choice (APA Press 2011);

Rambachan, Anantanand, Like a Ripe Fruit Separating Effortlessly from Its Vine, in Harold Coward & Kelli I. Stajduhar, eds., Religious Understandings of a Good Death in Palliative Care (SUNY Press 2012);

Ravvin, Norman, Traditions and Change in Jewish Ideals Regarding a Good Death, in Harold Coward & Kelli I. Stajduhar, eds., Religious Understandings of a Good Death in Palliative Care (SUNY Press 2012);

Raz, Joseph, Death in Our Life (Oxford Legal Studies Research Paper No. 25/2012; Columbia Public Law Research Paper No. 12-305; May 29, 2012);

Rubin, Paul H., & Joanna Shepherd, Tort Reform and Accidental Deaths, 50 Journal of Law & Economics 221 (2007);

Sarat, Austin, Gruesome Spectacles: Botched Executions and America's Death Penalty (Stanford University Press 2014);

Sarat, Austin, ed., Pain, Death and the Law (University of Michigan Press 2001);

Schechtman, Marya, The Malleability of Identity, in Steven Luper, ed., The Cambridge Companion to Life and Death (Cambridge University Press 2014);

Schopenhauer, Arthur, On the Vanity of Existence, in E.D. Klemke, ed., The Meaning of Life (Oxford University Press 2000);

Sekeles, Chava, Music Therapy: Death and Grief (Barcelona Publishers 2007);

Sherry, Kristina, What Happens to Our Facebook Accounts When We Die?: Probate Versus Policy and the Fate of Social-Media Assets Postmortem, 40 Pepperdine 184 (2013);

Sinclair, Shane, & Harvey Chochinov, Research and Practice: Spiritual Perspectives of a Good Death within Evidence-Based Health Care, in Paul Bramadat, Harold Coward, & Kelli I. Stajduhar, Spirituality in Hospice and Palliative Care (SUNY Press 2013);

Sneddon, Karen J., Speaking for the Dead: Voice in Last Wills and Testaments, 85 St. John's Law Review 683 (2011);

Soskice, Janet, Dying Well in Christianity, Harold Coward & Kelli I. Stajduhar, eds., Religious Understandings of a Good Death in Palliative Care (SUNY Press 2012);

Souza, Margaret, When the Poor Get More, in Christina Staudt & Marcelline Block, eds., Unequal Before Death (Cambridge Scholars Publishing 2012);

Spellman, W.M., A Brief History of Death (Reaktion Books 2014);

Spiro, Howard, Lee Palmer Wandel, & Mary G. McCrea Curnen, eds., Facing Death: Where Culture, Religion, and Medicine Meet (Yale University Press 1998);

Staudt, Christina, & Marcelline Block, eds., Unequal Before Death (Cambridge Scholars Publishing 2012);

Steffen, Lloyd, Stop the Killing, in Christina Staudt & Marcelline Block, eds., Unequal Before Death (Cambridge Scholars Publishing 2012);

Strobel, Lee, The Case for Christ: A Journalist's Personal Investigation of the Evidence for Jesus (Zondervan 1998);

Sunstein, Cass, & Adrian Vermeule, Is Capital Punishment Morally Required? The Relevance of Life-Life Tradeoffs (University of Chicago Law & Economics Olin Working Paper No. 239, March 2005);

Teresi, Dick, The Undead: Organ Harvesting, the Ice-Water Test, Beating-Heart Cadavers—How Medicine Is Blurring the Line Between Life and Death (Vintage Books 2012);

Townsend, Chris, Art and Death (I.B. Tauris 2008);

Ventry, Dennis J., Straight Talk About the Death Tax: Politics, Economics, and Morality, 89 Tax Notes 1159 (November 27, 2000);

Vidal, Ricarda, The Power of Negative Creation—Why Art by Serial Killers Sells, in Maria-Jose Blanco & Ricarda Vidal, eds., The Power of Death: Contemporary Reflections on Death in Western Society (Berghann 2014);

Viscusi, W. Kip, The Value of Life (New Palgrave Dictionary of Economics and the Law 2d ed., Vanderbilt Law & Economics Research Paper No. 08-04, October 14, 2005);

Warraich, Haider, Modern Death: How Medicine Changed the End of Life (St. Martin's Press 2017);

Warren, James, Facing Death: Epicurus and His Critics (Clarendon Press 2004);

Warren, James, Symmetry Problem, in Steven Luper, ed., The Cambridge Companion to Life and Death (Cambridge University Press 2014);

Waugh, Earle, Muslim Perspectives on a Good Death in Hospice and End-of-Life Care, in Harold Coward & Kelli I. Stajduhar, eds., Religious Understandings of a Good Death in Palliative Care (SUNY Press 2012);

Willard, Dallas, The Divine Conspiracy: Rediscovering Our Hidden Life in God (Harper San Francisco 1998);

Wolf, Susan M., Pragmatism in the Face of Death: The Role of Facts in the Assisted Suicide Debate, 82 Minnesota Law Review 1063 (1998);

Woods, Cathal, & Ryan Pack, trans., Socrates' Defense (The Apology of Socrates) (Creative Commons 2007-2016);

Wright, Michael, & David Clark, Cicely Saunders and the Development of Hospice Palliative Care, in Harold Coward & Kelli I. Stajduhar, eds., Religious Understandings of a Good Death in Palliative Care (SUNY Press 2012).

About the Author

Nelson Miller is a professor and associate dean at Western Michigan University Thomas M. Cooley Law School. Dean Miller practiced civil litigation for seventeen years in a small-firm setting, representing individuals, corporations, agencies, and public and private universities, before moving to teaching thirteen years ago. He has published thirty-six books and dozens of book chapters and articles on law, faith, and education. The State Bar of Michigan recognized Dean Miller with the John W. Cummiskey Award for pro-bono service.

www.ingramcontent.com/pod-product-compliance
Lightning Source LLC
Chambersburg PA
CBHW070611300426
44113CB00010B/1492